The media's wat
Here's a sampling of our coverage.

"Unflinching, fly-on-the-wall reports... No one gets past company propaganda to the nitty-gritty inside dope better than these guys."
— *Knight-Ridder newspapers*

"Best way to scope out potential employers...Vault has sharp insight into corporate culture and hiring practices."
— *Yahoo! Internet Life*

"Vault has become a de facto Internet outsourcer of the corporate grapevine."
— *Fortune*

"For those hoping to climb the ladder of success, [Vault's] insights are priceless."
— *Money.com*

"Another killer app for the Internet."
— *New York Times*

"If only the company profiles on the top sites would list the 'real' information... Sites such as Vault do this, featuring insights and commentary from employees and industry analysts."
— *The Washington Post*

"A rich repository of information about the world of work."
— *Houston Chronicle*

VAULT CAREER GUIDE TO MEDIA & ENTERTAINMENT

© 2003 Vault Inc.

VAULT CAREER GUIDE TO MEDIA & ENTERTAINMENT

SUCHARITA MULPURU
AND THE STAFF OF VAULT

© 2003 Vault Inc.

Copyright © 2003 by Vault Inc. All rights reserved.

All information in this book is subject to change without notice. Vault makes no claims as to the accuracy and reliability of the information contained within and disclaims all warranties. No part of this book may be reproduced or transmitted in any form or by any means, electronic or mechanical, for any purpose, without the express written permission of Vault Inc.

Vault, the Vault logo, and "the insider career network™" are trademarks of Vault Inc.

For information about permission to reproduce selections from this book, contact Vault Inc., 150 W. 22nd St., 5th Floor, New York, NY 10011, (212) 366-4212.

Library of Congress CIP Data is available.

ISBN 1-58131-200-8

Printed in the United States of America

ACKNOWLEDGEMENTS

Thanks to everyone who had a hand in making this book possible, especially Marcy Lerner, Ed Shen, Jake Wallace and Kelly Shore. We are also extremely grateful to Vault's entire staff of writers, editors and interns for all their help in the editorial and production processes.

Vault also would like to acknowledge the support of Matt Doull, Ahmad Al-Khaled, Lee Black, Eric Ober, Hollinger Ventures, Tekbanc, New York City Investment Fund, Globix, Hoover's, Glenn Fischer, Mark Hernandez, Ravi Mhatre, Carter Weiss, Ken Cron, Ed Somekh, Isidore Mayrock, Zahi Khouri, Sana Sabbagh, and other Vault investors, as well as our family and friends.

Sucharita's acknowledgements:

To my numerous friends currently in and formerly of the entertainment industry, who provided me invaluable insights and splendid stories that colored the pages of this book-in particular, Julie Appiah, Deb Cincotta, Chad Hazelton, Rachel Huston, Patty Kao, Michele Kawamoto and Laurie McCartney; to many former colleagues, creative executives from Brillstein-Grey, Imagine Entertainment and others, and lecturers from the UCLA film school, who gave me time and suggestions on the intricacies of this business; to refugees from the media industry who also happened to be classmates at Stanford Business School and gave me countless brilliant suggestions on the advice to give aspiring moguls--especially Jeremie Sokolowsky of the Arts, Media & Entertainment Club, Claire Ellis, Sally Wolf, Liz Michaels and Stephanie Schwartz. And of course, my most gratitude for which words are insufficient to my father, mother, Shanti and Sesi for their tireless support of this endeavor and all others.

Table of Contents

INTRODUCTION 1

THE SCOOP 3

The Industry 5
Motion Pictures 5
Television 7
Publishing 9
Music 11
Media Conglomerate Relationships 13
Case Study: Music Industry Internet Strategy .13

Trends in Media & Entertainment 15
Case Study: The Video Game Industry 18

GETTING HIRED 19

The Big Conundrums 21
New York or Los Angeles? 21
Creative or Business? 21
The Role of Education 22
Choosing an Industry 23
Vault Expert Advice: Choosing a Magazine 24

The Business Side: Hiring 27
Breaking In 27
Our Survey Says: Lifestyle and Pay 31
Typical Career Path 33
The Interview 34
Sample Questions and Answers 34
Things to Watch Out For 36

The Creative Side: Hiring 39

Breaking In 39
Our Survey Says: Lifestyle and Pay 43
Typical Career Path 46
The Interview 47
Sample Questions and Answers 47
Things to Watch Out For 48

ON THE JOB 51

The Business Side: The Jobs 53

Strategic Planning 53
Corporate Finance 54
Corporate Marketing 56
Corporate Public Relations 56
Internet Strategy 57
Real Estate Development 57
Home Video Management 58
Consumer Products Licensing 59
Retail Stores Development 60
Theme Parks Management 60
Film Distribution and Theater Management 63
Accounting 65
Human Resources 65
Information Technology 65
Legal 65
Organizational Chart of Media Companies 66
A Day in the Life of an Inventory Planning Manager 68
A Day in the Life of a Strategic Planning Entertainment Executive 69
Vault Expert Advice: Media MBAs 71

The Creative Side: The Jobs 75

Studios – Development 75
Producer 76
Studios – Marketing 77
Entertainment Publicist 78

Talent Agent 78
Director 79
Web Designer 80
Post Production 80
Crew 81
A Day in the Life of a Creative Executive 83
Creative Assistant 85
Screenwriter 85
Script Reader 85
Trade Publishing Editor 86
TV Programming 86
A Day in the Life of a Network News Producer 87
A&R Rep 88
A Day in the Life of a Senior News Editor, Major News Magazine 88
How a Movie Gets Made 91

Survival Skills for Assistants   93

Getting In 93
The Interview 93
Managing Your Boss 94
Making the Most of Low Wages 95
Getting Promoted 95
Vault Expert Advice: Becoming a Magazine Editorial Assistant 96

Dream Jobs   105

Independent Film Producer 105
Senior Vice President, Major Entertainment Studio 106
Assistant Publisher, Major Women's Magazine 107
Literary Agent 108
Screenwriter 109

APPENDIX 111

FAQ 113

Glossary and Industry Jargon 117

Employer Index 121

Miscellaneous Media 121
Gaming 123
TV Networks 124
Movie Studies and Music Labels 125
Talent Agencies 126
Movie Theater Companies 127
Production Companies 128
Publishing Houses 129

Recommended Reading and Other Sources 131

About the Author 137

Introduction

CHAPTER 1

Ready for your close-up?

Whether it is the love of television and movies, or a keen interest in celebrities and hot Hollywood hangouts, or even dreams of Oscar ovations, Malibu mansions and chic restaurant reservations, you've probably been bitten by the entertainment bug. And you're not alone. Every year, tens of thousands of newcomers, all optimistically hoping to be players, arrive in New York and Los Angeles in search of the lights, camera and action of the entertainment industry.

The media and entertainment industry encompass an enormous spectrum of jobs in both creative and business capacities. Opportunities abound in everything from orchestrating the music in a major motion picture to orchestrating the mergers and acquisitions of media conglomerates. There are hundreds of people who are critical to the creation of any creative property – just look at the acknowledgments in a CD cover, the credits at the end of a TV or movie, the masthead in a magazine, not to mention the myriads of other worker bees behind the scenes who are never acknowledged.

This translates to literally hundreds of types of jobs. Yet media and entertainment is a tough industry to break into because it is so insular. Jobs are scarce, turnover is high and relatively few ever make it big. Life in Hollywood is often, in the words of Hobbes, "nasty, brutish and short."

But while personal networks are tight and tough to penetrate and the work is often long and tiresome, fortune and glory await those who are able to successfully navigate the many obstacles.

In this Vault Guide, we'll walk you through what you can expect from the different jobs in the industry and what you can do to get yourself in the door (and up the ladder). There are also several case studies throughout the book that are real-life examples of problems and solutions facing executives at some leading media and entertainment companies.

This book treats separately each of the two parts of the industry: the creative side (those that create the content) and the business side (those that sell it, orchestrating the money-making, the marketing and distribution of the creative content). The major mediums within media and entertainment that we will cover in this guide include motion pictures and television, with some attention to the music industry and publishing. We'll give overviews of it all, and our thoughts on what it may hold for you.

Good luck! Now, quiet on the set…

THE SCOOP

Chapter 2: The Industry

Chapter 3: Trends in Media & Entertainment

The Industry

CHAPTER 2

The media universe is dotted with veritable galaxies of companies – from multi-billion dollar diversified conglomerates to small, independent movie studios and production facilities. High school dropouts and PhDs in philosophy, MBAs and computer programmers, septuagenarians and twentysomethings, all work cheek by jowl to bring to life creative endeavors, to grow sustainable billion-dollar franchises like *Batman* and *Harry Potter*, and to create new ways to keep the American public entertained and spending money on leisure.

There are two broad subcategories within media and entertainment: creative and business. The creative side actually makes the products or content and has four major areas: motion pictures, television, publishing and music. The business side sells the content, ensures that everything is legal and helps the business grow. The business encompasses the corporate high-level strategy groups, the divisions (a.k.a. business units) that work in the trenches of a specific operation and the standard overarching business functions evident in every company (e.g. accounting, legal, human resources, IT).

First and foremost, entertainment and media industries start with creative content. Everything else stems from this. (See the chart on Media Companies for a graphic overview at the end of this chapter.)

Motion Pictures

Movies are by far the biggest segment of the media and entertainment industry, not only because of their prominence within the American cultural landscape, but also because of a successful motion picture's ability to sell products in other enormously profitable places as well (also known as ancillary revenue streams) – home video, international distribution, TV rights and so on. Each of the eight major film studios releases about 20 to 30 films each year, with the average studio release costing about $30 million. Studios are typically broken down into two functional components, the business side and the creative side.

The creative side is the where the movies are actually made. There are a few key divisions on the creative side of the movie business:

- **Development:** The key players in the development stage are producers, screenwriters, agents and studio executives. Production companies, the "homes" of producers, start with a script. Every year, these companies are delivered hundreds of scripts (mostly unsolicited) from famous, semi-famous and unknown writers. The executives at each of the production companies then sort through the scripts (written by both new and established screenwriters), negotiate with agents to purchase interesting ones, and then bring together key players (e.g. a director, lead actors, other producers) who will commit to starring in or making the film if a studio finances it. A studio is then "pitched" the idea and if the film is approved, the film then gets a "green light" to go into production. The latter stage of development is also often called pre-production.

- **Pre-production:** This is everything that happens to get a movie rolling just before filming starts – location scouting, and the casting and hiring of the crew, for instance.

- **Production:** Once a movie is "green lit," production starts. To use an analogy, if the screenplay is the blueprint, production is when the movie is built by the cast and crew. Filming sometimes happens on a soundstage on a film studio's property, but often it occurs "on location," at an out-of-studio venue.

> **Top Studios**
> - Disney
> - Dreamworks SKG
> - MGM/UA
> - Paramount
> - Sony/Columbia
> - Universal
> - Warner Brothers
> - 20th Century Fox
>
> **Top "Indy" Studios**
> - Artisan
> - Fine Line/New Line
> - Fox Searchlight
> - Miramax
> - Sony Pictures Classics
> - USA Films

- **Post-Production:** After all the raw footage has been filmed, it is taken to an editing studio, where professional film editors and the director work together with sound effects artists and special effects wizards (if necessary) to pull a movie together. This is also the stage when music, titles and credits are added and when the film preview (called a "trailer" in industry-speak) is created and sent to movie theaters.

Vital in the movie business is the relationship that studios have with movie theaters, or exhibitors, as they are called in the industry. Exhibitors decide which movies they will show and often split marketing costs with theaters. Because of the 1948 antitrust ruling that divorced theaters from studios, the power of studios weakened. Multiplexes (cinema theaters with multiple screens) then came into the picture, taking advantage of the separation from studios to release many different types of movies, contributing to the proliferation of movie niches and independent films produced on small budgets.

The other side of filmmaking is the business side, which deals with ancillary revenue streams and creative vehicles (e.g., theme parks, licensed products, home video) that come after the filmmaking process. These are often completely separate businesses that employ different media for dissemination (e.g., stores, third party distributors like McDonald's, the Internet). Because many of the most successful movies of all time are franchises (*Star Wars*, *Indiana Jones*, *Lord of the Rings*), the business side works to exploit the enormous revenue opportunities that come with leveraging those properties. As the business side has come to generate billions of dollars in recent years, movie studios have grown into diversified conglomerates with many different business arms. The main divisions are:

- **Home video:** Tapes and DVDs are the second phase of a movie's life cycle, bringing films into the homes of consumers after its life in the box office has run its course.

- **Consumer products:** All filmed properties and characters with commercial appeal are further exploited by other companies that pay licensing fees for the rights to use images and names.

- **Retail:** Virtually all major film studios sell customized items directly to customers either through stores, catalogs or direct mail, some in larger endeavors than others (e.g. The Disney Stores, Warner Brothers Studio Stores).

- **Theme parks:** Large destination parks (e.g. Disneyland, Universal Studios) provide the opportunity to further leverage a film's appeal to consumers in an exciting, live-action setting.

Television

With televisions in the homes of over 99% of the U.S. population, TV is arguably the most powerful media vehicle in the entertainment industry. Deregulation of cable companies and increased bandwidth in distribution (with digital cable) has further increased the options of television networks. This has resulted in a glut of channels targeting ever-narrower niches (e.g. golf, cooking, independent movies).

This growth, however, has resulted in the popularity of several successful cable channels eroding the once dominant share of the networks (ABC, CBS, NBC). Success stories include ESPN, E!, Lifetime, USA and MTV. One result of all this change is the growth in career opportunities for people considering television careers.

The TV industry is structured somewhat differently from film. One of the key difference is that TV is full of sales and marketing positions, since most networks make money on advertising. (If a show is particularly successful, it can make even more money by being sold into syndication (e.g., *Law & Order*), by being made into a movie (e.g., *The X-Files*) or by launching spin-offs (e.g., *Cheers* launching *Frasier*). Typically, the network does not make much money from these types of deals; the winners are usually the creators of the show and the production company that originally produced the show. Advertising, therefore, is all the more critical for networks.

Top TV Networks

ABC	USA
NBC	ESPN
CBS	A&E
Fox	CNN
PBS	TNT
TBS	Nickelodeon
Discovery	Lifetime

Here are some key divisions of television networks:

- **Development:** The television industry parallels the film industry in that scripts for new television shows are constantly sought out and studied in the hopes of creating the next *Friends* or *ER*. Job positions within TV development are typically divided into the different types of programming that appears on TV – sitcoms, dramas, miniseries, specials and daytime. Network executives are "pitched" ideas by production companies and writers. If the executive likes an idea, a "green light" is given for the show's pilot, the introductory episode. If the pilot is successful, it then becomes a series.

- **Production:** Because television typically calls for shorter production cycles, television studios are often fully equipped soundstages where TV shows are filmed and edited and where final cuts are put into post-production.

- **Programming:** Once a show is on the air, it is watched carefully to see how it performs. Programming executives closely monitor Nielsen ratings, provide comments on scripts to develop shows with the most promising audience appeal, reconfigure schedules to improve performances and cut shows when they fail to build a loyal audience. Shows may be kept when their ratings are low but they attract the desirable 18- to 34-year-old audience.

- **Network affiliates:** While the bulk of ad revenues come in at the national level, the major networks have bodies of network affiliates throughout the country that have individual sales forces that sell local advertising, which comprises most of the remaining portion of overall company revenues. In addition to ad sales, affiliates also manage some content creation, primarily local news production.

Publishing

While the overall revenue from publishing is dwarfed by film and television, books and magazines occupy a place of cultural significance in America that is unparalleled. The trade book industry (that is, all the mass market fiction and non-fiction books that you see in the bookstore, as opposed to academic textbooks and journals) is one of the most important sources of story ideas; in the film world books are constantly being brought to life as movies. Likewise, magazines are also important because they illustrate cultural trends and societal shifts, raise intriguing questions that become hot topics-du-jour, and are able to market businesses more effectively than most forms of advertising.

Top Trade Publishers
- Bantam Doubleday Dell
- Harcourt Brace
- HarperCollins
- Hyperion
- Little
- Brown
- W.W. Norton
- William Morrow
- Putnam Berkley
- Penguin
- Random House
- Simon & Schuster
- St. Martin's Press
- Warner Books

Trade and magazine publishing is similar to both film and TV in that the former makes money from direct sales while the latter makes money based on advertising and overall circulation.

The key divisions of trade publishing houses are:

- **Editorial:** Editors receive raw manuscripts from literary agents, decide what gets published in their annual roster and work to shape the text into a commercially viable form.

- **Publicity:** Since book sales are largely dependent on word of mouth, publicity becomes an extremely important part of a book's success. Book publicists orchestrate book tours, bookstore signings, live readings by the author, appearances on television programs, press releases and press kits, and place reviews in publications.

- **Marketing:** Book marketers work with graphic designers and artists to create book jackets and ads, and work with programs like book-of-the-month clubs in order to promote sales. They also create in-store shelf displays for bookstores to help sell books.

- **Operations:** Many major book publishers have their own printing presses and warehouses, where they can ship directly to key bookstores (like Barnes & Noble and Borders) and distributors (like Ingram).

- **Distribution:** A crucial component of a book's sale process is getting the book distributed to both chain and independent bookstores. Publishers have representatives at headquarters who work with the largest chains to place books, signage and displays, as well as regional representatives who pitch, promote and sell books to smaller independent bookstores. Distribution's key objective is to ensure placement and instant availability of books in the retail channels where consumers seek product.

The key divisions of a magazine publisher are:

- **Editorial:** Magazine editors are often given credit for determining a publication's "voice." Magazine editors determine what goes on the cover and manage writers (both full-time staff writers as well as freelancers), photographers, artists and graphic designers. The editorial team has responsibility for the overall editorial calendar, which is the list of upcoming stories that is provided to advertisers who may wish to run ads in a particular issue to target a particular sub-segment of an audience.

- **Advertising sales:** Magazine salespeople work with major advertising agencies and their clients. Much schmoozing is involved in the sale of ads.

Top Magazine Publishers
- Time Inc.
- The Washington Post Co.
- Forbes
- Hearst
- Hachette Filipacci
- Gruner & Jahr
- Martha Stewart
- Conde Nast
- Wenner Media
- Primedia
- Weider
- American Express Publishing
- Ziff Davis

- **Distribution/Circulation/Marketing:** A magazine is able to command ad rates depending on how broad its circulation is, who subscribes to the magazine and who ultimately sees each issue (the "pass-through rate"). This department is primarily involved with maintaining subscriptions, attracting subscriptions through direct mail and other marketing, distributing free copies to appropriate channels and increasing the number of 'eyeballs' that view each issue.

Because most publishing headquarters are in New York, a career in the industry almost certainly means living in New York City.

Music

The music industry has several components – there are divisions that discover new artists, there are those that develop and produce music with mass appeal, and there are the promoters and marketers. And now, in the age of the Internet, there are lots of people hired to make sure that the record labels do not get fleeced by music freeloaders who find ways to acquire and disseminate the product for free, or to figure out how to create profitable businesses distributing or marketing music through the Internet.

Big 5 Record Labels
- BMG (Arista, Jive Records, RCA)
- EMI-Capitol (Virgin)
- Sony (Columbia, Epic)
- Universal (MCA, Polygram)
- Warner (Warner Brothers, Elektra, Atlantic)

While the music industry is enormous, and one of the most globally-significant parts of the entertainment industry because music is so universal and ubiquitous, the threat of its erosion due to Internet piracy concerns poses a serious threat to the growth of new artists and revenue opportunities.

That said, for job seekers, the most promising opportunities continue to be in A&R, distribution and marketing.

- **A&R:** These are the talent scouts that listen to demo tapes, attend shows, travel and keep their ear to the ground to understand new trends and to uncover fresh voices that best bring those trends to life.
- **Production:** Once an act has been signed onto a record label, the producers perfect the music to make it commercially palatable for radio stations, critics and consumers. The packaging of the CD and creation of the artist image is also finalized in this stage.

- **PR/Marketing:** This is the group that toils to get airplay on radio stations, gets the music video shot and hopefully aired, leverages television and press coverage and puts the artist in the public eye. Arbitron ratings, essentially Nielsen ratings for radio, let both radio stations and record labels know what consumers are listening to, what is working and what is most popular.

- **Distribution:** This group specifically deals with getting the CDs into record stores and venues where consumers can purchase them.

- **Concerts:** Concerts and live performances that are able to attract large numbers of consumers are increasingly underwritten by large corporate sponsors to defray expenses (e.g., Pepsi sponsoring a Britney Spears concert tour).

The biggest media companies (i.e. AOL Time Warner, Viacom, The Walt Disney Company, Viacom) span across all of these industries (and then some). The chart on the next page shows roughly how these large organizations are structured.

Vault Career Guide to Media & Entertainment
The Industry

Media Conglomerate Relationships

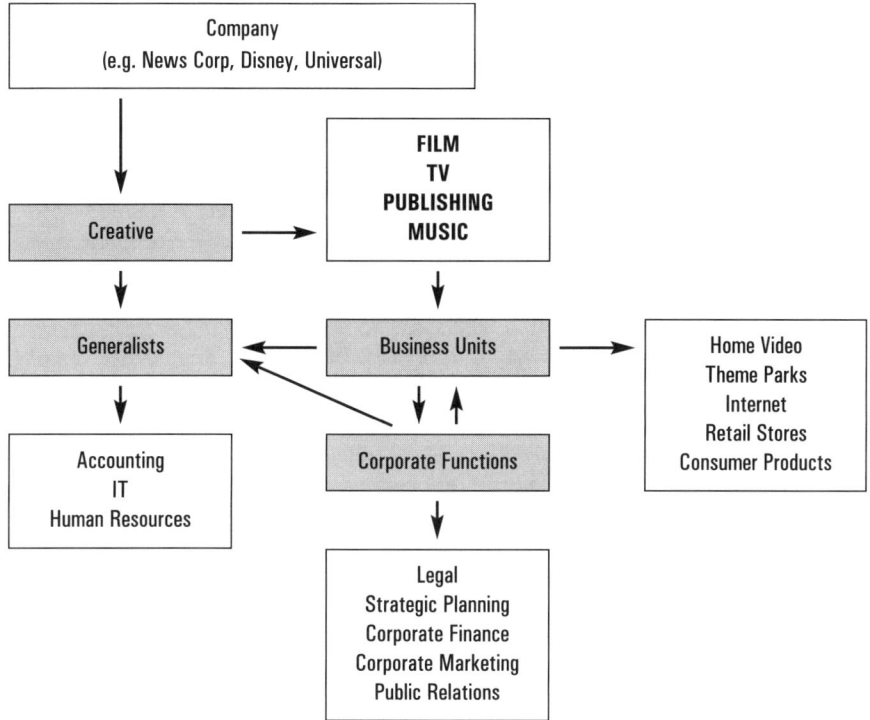

Case Study: Music Industry, Internet Strategy

Company: Bertelsmann Group (BMG)

Division: Strategic Planning

Project: To create an Internet strategy that tackled the challenges of competing with free music distribution occurring through sources like Napster.

BMG is one of the world's largest producers of music. In the mid-1990s however, with the advent of the Internet and the widespread popularity of MP3s, BMG and the entire music industry felt a seismic shift that could damage their future revenue streams.

BMG, like the other large music labels, felt threatened by the digital distribution of music through illicit, difficult-to-track means like file-sharing services. All the major music companies were deeply concerned with this issue. As digital music distribution became more prominent and popular, the music companies were forced to fight to protect their cash machines.

BMG was one of the first labels to invest in an e-commerce platform of its own, to investigate streaming opportunities and to inquire into options for leveraging this new medium. It soon became evident that the medium could do quite a bit of harm to the company's revenue stream and intellectual property.

Over the course of several years in the mid-1990s, one of the major corporate-wide initiatives of the company was to examine if there was a way to both develop internal security systems to prevent the reproduction of content, and to investigate new and emerging revenue streams that could replace or supplement the purchase of CDs and recorded music in record stores. A special Internet group, comprised of many leaders from the executive ranks of the company as well as their newly hired MBAs, was created precisely to address this issue.

Massive efforts were spent on copyright protection, as well as both engineering and legal fees to bring the music business to the next frontier. Some of the tasks of this group included:

- Working with software companies to understand upcoming technologies that could avert the distribution of free music;

- Collaborating with venture capitalists and other investors in cutting-edge security technology;

- Evaluating potential acquisition candidates;

- Creating an overarching strategy to address BMG's role within the music industry.

For Bertelsmann, the end result was the cash infusion into and eventual purchase of file-sharing web site Napster. Given Napster's cessation of operations and the emergence of other similar operations, the problem still continues; Bertelsmann continues to investigate options to address this issue.

Trends in Media & Entertainment

CHAPTER 3

There are numerous shifts in the delivery and creation of content that will affect the media and entertainment industry in coming years and provide new, non-traditional job opportunities. Here we'll take a look at some of the most prominent of these trends.

Preprogramming gives way to video/music-on-demand

One studio exec confides, "Video on demand (VOD) has been our biggest initiative for the last three years and will continue to be so. This will determine how the next generation of content delivery will be produced." On-demand entertainment is basically the next step beyond pay-per-view, when an individual can see or hear anything he or she wants, at any time, without having to use a VCR, an alarm clock or even Tivo. (Tivo is a product that attaches to a TV and allows its owner to record any show at any time without a timer or cassette.) While video-on-demand experiments have been launched unsuccessfully in recent years, the conventional wisdom is that they failed because the technology had not caught up to the concept. There is increasing evidence that VOD will be a critical part of all digital subscriber packages of the future, in which case it will represent a tremendous shift in the current revenue stream of content providers.

Creative endeavors are saturated with special effects

Special effects in movies are increasingly sophisticated. The growth of companies like LucasFilm's Industrial Light and Magic (ILM), Pixar, Silicon Graphics and others, means that entertainment is increasingly blurring the line between creativity and engineering. Some movies, like the Oscar-nominated *Toy Story*, are one huge special effect. Other popular franchises, like *Harry Potter* and the *Lord of the Rings*, are effects-heavy. One employee at ILM remarked, "Five years ago when I started, there was one other person in my group (business development) – now there are about 30." Some companies to watch: Pixar, LucasFilm, and Blue Skye, the maker of the surprise animated Fox hit, *Ice Age*.

Micromarketing drives the best advertising models

With the explosion of cable networks and the existence of countless niches within publishing and on the Web, it is now possible to target prospective clients more precisely than ever before. One negative repercussion is that it puts more pressure on major networks like NBC and ABC to squeeze more revenue out of their remaining mass market products. On the positive side, there are more opportunities for consultants and marketers who can address the needs of target audiences.

Glocalization allows globalization

Glocalization is the micro-specialization within certain countries, cultures, regions or markets of mass products available elsewhere. One popular example is MTV, which tailors its programming with native language music and personalities in Latin America, China and India. While localizing content seems an obvious part of entering foreign markets, it is still something that is often neglected. The next century will likely change that, especially as major entertainment companies expand to other markets through acquisitions, alliances with local players and Web portals targeted to regional markets.

Hollywood continues to court big business

While content is the bread-and-butter of media and entertainment companies, content is also hit-driven and cyclical in nature. To provide a steady cash flow, companies rely on corporate sponsorships to provide regular revenue streams. The magazine publishing and television industries have relied on this revenue stream for years, and film and music are quickly joining them. It all started with legendary (and now deposed) agent Michael Ovitz of Creative Artists Agency who signed Coca-Cola as a corporate client back in the mid-1980s.

For Coke, CAA was responsible for strategic marketing and some advertising. More importantly, CAA provided Coke with access to celebrities, spokespeople and key cultural influencers who could provide brand endorsements in an increasingly competitive marketing environment. In addition to providing celebrity affiliations, agencies were also known for providing entrée into event marketing, the requisite Hollywood parties, meetings and shows. For CAA, this 'branching out' provided credibility as it was now legitimately entrusted with brokering bona fide business deals (not to mention collecting consistent paychecks). All in all, it was a win-win for both sides. For job seekers, this means that there are more non-traditional business opportunities for enterprising MBAs with an interest in merging an interest in entertainment and business.

The video gaming industry gets bigger

As technology advances, so do video games, which are already a multi-billion dollar industry. Many franchises within entertainment have proven that a popular character can create billions for a company, and video games are no exception to that rule. "This is perhaps the biggest growth engine in the entire entertainment industry," said one investment analyst covering media companies. Some companies to watch: Activision, Eidos, Electronic Arts, Infogrames, Midway, THQ, Take Two.

Case Study: The Video Game Industry

Company: Sony

Division: Video Games

Project: To create a new revenue stream to supplement the wildly popular PlayStation2.

For years, Sony has been an extremely successful entertainment and electronics company. In 2001 alone, over $57 billion in revenue was generated by sales of Walkmans, Trinitrons, Vaios and PlayStations. However, the margins on these products have been increasingly eroded and in the challenge was particularly fierce in the video game space. The once-inimitable Sony PlayStation2 was facing stiff competition from Microsoft which was pricing its XBox far below cost.

Senior management sought to find a way to utilize the company's tremendous engineering resources and create a product that could salvage its revenue potential. With the growing penetration of more powerful PCs both at home and at work, executives at Sony had a hunch that a foray into online video games could work.

The first step was to ask analysts within the video game division to assess how much it would cost to create this capability in-house. The result was not promising; a typical game costs $2 million, but creating something online would cost twice that much. Sony eventually executed a deal with a senior engineer, who was given money to create a separate company to create the software on his own, in exchange for partial ownership of the end product.

The opinions of business development executives and senior marketers were solicited throughout the course of the project, both to assess the market potential of this new "online multiplayer model" and to discover the elements that would give the product mass appeal. The individuals were entrusted with finding who played various types of games, who would pay for the service in a subscription model, how much they would pay, and what would bring consumers back for more.

The result was Sony EverQuest. EverQuest is a shared, vaguely medieval universe where players can do everything from run taverns to kill monsters for treasure. It's sometimes called "EverCrack" because the social and game aspects are so compelling and addictive. By mid-2002, the product attracted 500,000 subscribers who each pay $12.95 per month. In the first few months of operation, the product was able to pay off its development costs, a home run by any measure of business. Today, EQ (as it's sometimes called) can be played on handheld devices so that its loyal subscribers need not miss a moment.

GETTING HIRED

Chapter 4: The Big Conundrums

Chapter 5: The Business Side: Hiring

Chapter 6: The Creative Side: Hiring

The Big Conundrums

CHAPTER 4

In choosing to enter the entertainment industry, there are several personal decisions that you need to carefully consider. There are no "right" answers. Starting a career in entertainment often calls for steadfast commitment and patience. Some of these decisions involve location, others involve education, still others involve the line of business one can pursue.

New York or Los Angeles?

Most entertainment companies are situated on either the East or West Coast, and that is, by and large, where most newcomers end up. "You definitely want to start in New York or Los Angeles – it's where all the action is," were the words of one record label executive at Virgin. Los Angeles has the development and distribution arms of all the major film and television studios as well as many of the top offices of music labels as well. New York has the balance of the music business, as well as some television (MTV and Nickelodeon for example) and almost 90 percent of all the publishing powerhouses.

Increasingly though, the media and entertainment industry offers opportunities beyond New York and L.A. There are now far more businesses located in other parts of the United States and the world, especially as production costs soar in New York and L.A. Canada is increasingly popular with movie studios, and Vancouver and Toronto both have thriving arts communities. Likewise, the concentration of software engineers in Silicon Valley makes it the home of many special effects companies. Cable networks are increasingly located away from major cities, and shows are often shot in studios in smaller cities like Atlanta and New Orleans. In fact, the most music production outside of New York and Los Angeles occurs in Nashville, the home of the ever-popular country music genre.

Creative or business?

While the creative side of the entertainment business is often considered more interesting because it is what encourages creativity (and because it is the side that holds the best parties with all the famous celebrities), the compensation is lower, the career trajectory is less certain and the work, especially initially, can be demeaning. Assistants often work 12 hours a day, endure being yelled at regularly and must often trek around town every morning to fetch their boss' coffee, dry-cleaned clothes and children.

The business side, on the other hand, is generally regarded as less exciting. There is a fair amount of showmanship even in this part of the business (there was one such businessman who was legendary for keeping his "director-level" business card after being promoted to VP in the hopes that others would believe him to be a film director), but for the most part the path is more predictable, performance is rewarded and the pay is more generous. The tradeoff is, of course, that the positions are not glamorous and the hours are often just as long. "You always feel like you are on the periphery of where the action really is," laments one executive who works in a studio's home video division.

The choice is certainly a difficult one. Success is often not transferable. There are occasionally tales of the studio accountant who transitioned to be a TV producer, but in general, very few make lateral moves, especially since the work required to build up a creative resume is very different than for a business resume, and vice versa.

The role of education

The role of education in the success of Hollywood players remains an enigma. Insiders often say that their degree was worthless in landing their job. In general, the creative side does not reward MBAs. On the business side, however, a graduate degree is often a critical success factor. Furthermore, entrée into the business side of entertainment comes to many only because of an MBA – there are executive training programs at many top media companies (e.g. Bertelsmann, Sony, Disney, Random House) that recruit at many leading business schools. While these are competitive and coveted positions, there is enough to go around for the truly committed. One recent MBA graduate from a top program said, "I just moved to Los Angeles without a job and had interviews with everyone I knew for a month straight – informationals, job interviews, anyone who would talk to me." She eventually landed a promising manager-level position in television distribution.

On the creative side, there are a slew of hot directors and other moviemakers that hail from the ranks of the film school elite – New York University, the American Film Institute, UCLA, USC and others. While these schools offer strong alumni networks and thorough training, there are costly investments. In addition to the annual tuition of the program, there is the additional expense of creating one's final project – a film that will likely cost at least $20,000. There are many success stories of talented people who saved money by taking classes at local community colleges, rented cheap equipment and made their way to festivals like Sundance.

Choosing an industry

The decision on what industry to pursue depends on one's interests and passions. The industries are all similar – personalities drive the business, egos are enormous, attitudes are bad and expectations are high. There are important differences, however. Film and TV generally allow more transition between the two (writers, actors, directors, even producers switch between the two media), but for the most part, it is much harder to transition out of music or publishing.

The key questions to ask yourself:

- What medium do you prefer? Do you really love music? Are you a big film buff? Do you read 20 magazines a month?

- Do you enjoy the artistic or business dimension of a project?

- Can you handle working on a project for several years (as is common in the film and music industries) or do you prefer projects that have shorter production cycles (which you will find in television and magazine publishing)?

- Would you enjoy working with a set team (the creative department of a film studio) or setting up projects with new people (as on the production side of filmmaking)?

- Where do you know more people? Where could you leverage a personal or alumni network?

- Where do you want to live? Do you like city living? Do you mind driving or do you prefer walking?

Remember that there are the inevitable sub-specializations, much like a lawyer who focuses on criminal litigation or a doctor who is a radiologist. Music executives, for instance, are known for the genre of music they produce, and film producers are normally associated with a certain type of film.

Choosing a Magazine

by Sally Lourenco

Before you decide to embark on a career in magazines, ask yourself the following questions:

- Can you live on very little money?
- Can you work without benefits?
- Are you willing to spend two or more years in a job before getting the opportunity to express your creative ideas?
- Will you be happy working as someone's assistant – doing menial tasks like answering calls, making schedules and travel arrangements, and preparing expense reports – for two or more years?
- Can you work late nights, weekends, when you're sick, and with little vacation time?
- Do you consider yourself a creative person who thinks of story and visual ideas and themes in the abstract, and is constantly inspired by daily life, events and news?
- Do you regularly read books, newspapers and magazines?
- Are you willing to continue your education, whether on the job or in the form of an advanced degree to pursue your goal of being an editor, writer etc.?
- Are you thick skinned? Can you avoid taking things personally as you work towards a higher goal?
- Are you persistent? Will you do anything (ethical) and any amount of work to get where you want?

If you can answer "yes" to all of these questions, then you're ready to pursue a career in magazines and will no doubt be a success at it. If you have answered "no" to any of these, don't bother trying to convince yourself. You might want to take a look at related industries or positions – perhaps advertising, publicity, or marketing.

It's not all about the glamour

I have known too many young interns and aspiring editors who have been charmed by the seemingly glamorous, high profile lifestyles of jet-set editors mingling with celebrities and living a charmed life. If you look closely, however, you'll see that those very few editors that do live charmed lives have been around for many years, are brilliant and focused on what they do, know the business, know their readers, are innovators and have done enough schlepping and long hard nights to make cramming for finals look like spring break.

Know that as you start out, whether as an intern, an editorial assistant or a director's right hand, the closest you'll get to glamour is faxing it a document. So you'd better be certain that you are on the right track, or you'll just waste your time and end up changing directions.

Keep in mind what one tough college professor once told me: look to your left, look to your right, then behind you and in front of you. Three of those four people won't be here next year.

A good percentage of people that start in this business leave pretty quickly. Some realize that the business is not what they expected, some can't deal with the poor compensation and others can't deal with the humbling aspects. They move on. But the ones that stick it out have a lot to gain – if they're willing to put in some serious time.

Getting started

Before you start approaching the glossies, weeklies or other consumer publications, you have to examine your preferences and goals. Your job search will be more effective if you know what you want to do and can pinpoint the types of magazines you would like to work on.

Here are a few more questions to ask yourself:

Do you like to write stories in a news style or more conversational style?

This will determine whether you'd prefer a magazine like *Time* over something like *Elle* or *Vanity Fair*.

Do you prefer to develop story ideas instead of writing?

This is important because it decides whether you'll start on a writing career track or end up as an editor who assigns stories and develops relationships with writers.

What topics interest you?

Every magazine has its focus, whether it be relationships, music, fashion, arts, books, film, celebrity profiles, food, money, business, or something else. Think about what you reach for at a newsstand – what interests you as a reader.

Are you more interested in visuals?

There are a number of places where you could work with art, photographers or as a stylist within the editorial realm. It's important to know whether you'd prefer to work on shoots and develop relationships with photographers, agents and models or if you'd like to work in graphics, setting up layouts.

Once you've answered these questions, you should have a good idea of what types of magazines you'd like to work for and the specific career path that would suit you best. The next step is finding the information to help you get where you want to go. It's not easy to find, but it is out there. It's up to you to do the legwork.

The Business Side: Hiring

CHAPTER 5

The media and entertainment industry can be divided into two broad subcategories: the creative side and the business side. The creative side is the part that creates the content – the magazine editors, the filmmakers and directors, the network executives, the music producers. The business side markets, sells and distributes the content, and orchestrates the overall rainmaking by marketing and distributing the content. This side includes the marketers, the business development executives, the salespeople and dealmakers. (For specific details of day-to-day responsibilities of jobs within the creative and business side, see Chapter 7.)

Landing any job in media and entertainment requires dedication, persistence and resilience. But don't think that landing a job on one side translates into success for the other. The skills to succeed are different and the so-called secrets of successful infiltration are quite dissimilar.

Breaking In

Background and qualifications

There is no set path to getting a business-side media job. Some things help, however. It helps to have graduated from a top university. It helps to have performed well in school or in previous jobs. You should have a passion for the industry. You should exhibit a fair degree of knowledge on the issues confronting entertainment companies (see The Interview section for specific questions to expect).

Post-College: There are a handful of analyst-level positions in entertainment companies. More common than positions for fresh college graduates are "industry hires" – young twentysomethings with a couple of years of experience under their belts in the professional services world, usually from top tier management consulting firms or banks, who can then be hired into business positions in the top entertainment companies. Because these strategic groups are small, positions for new professional hires are difficult to come by. But they do exist. Disney, Viacom and Universal all hire pre-MBA candidates.

Middle management: Other positions require some managerial experience, and sometimes an MBA. These positions involve managing operating units with profit and loss responsibility, supervising market research and due diligence in executing new ventures, and creating plans for future performance. While a background in entertainment may be useful, it is not necessary. Rather, experience in relevant industries (e.g. finance, marketing, operations) is arguably more critical.

The Competition

The business side of media and entertainment attracts a slew of different personality types. Among the most common characters are:

The Wannabe Player – the business person who really is a creative type at heart; often has plans (or sometimes just dreams) of transitioning to the creative side, usually has a screenplay or manuscript stashed in a desk somewhere.

The Mogul-to-Be – the hyper-ambitious young executives-in-the making aiming to be the next Rupert Murdoch, Sumner Redstone or Michael Eisner.

The Pit Stopper – young kids, often fresh out of college, anxious to check out the entertainment scene, but with no real passion to stay in the business long-term

The Transplant – usually a more seasoned senior executive who has been recruited from another company, presumably for his/her expertise.

Senior executive: While some companies are filled with people promoted from within, there is a fair amount of lateral hiring from other industries. Lateral hiring brings in fresh perspectives and also provides credibility to the investment community. These positions are often filled not through HR interviews, but through sophisticated, and often secretive, executive level headhunters and search firms like Heidrick & Struggles, Korn Ferry and Russell Reynolds. Many of these firms have specific media and entertainment practices.

Given however, that networking and schmoozing is such a critical component of getting in the door, there are some other avenues to explore. By and large, the best ways to make your own Rolodex of contacts are:

- **Recruiting at colleges and graduate programs.** This is by far the easiest way to get in the door if you can – recruiters are approaching your school with available jobs, giving you the opportunity to pitch yourself. Of course, you'll have a lot of competition. If possible, try to befriend other students at local universities like NYU or UCLA or USC where media job listings come through on a regular basis. They may have some options that are worth pursuing. One piece of advice by a recent MBA graduate: "Look for programs that recruit at colleges, universities and graduate schools, but not necessarily at your school – that could give you an extra edge you need to stand out from scores of other applicants all from your school."

- **Networking.** This is critical. There are numerous conferences that occur in Los Angeles and New York held by trade associations. Go and meet as many people as possible, speak to alumni, ask anyone who knows anyone if they can make a referral for you.

- **Trade publications.** The trades often have listings for positions at the corporate level for various jobs. And *Hollywood Reporter* and *Variety* are laden with news articles on who has left their job, who is new and what companies are expanding. Read the articles, glean some names and write some letters or make some calls

- **Headhunters.** There are some placement agencies that place everyone from junior managers to senior executives. They are found through Internet research, inquiring through friends and attending networking functions.

- **Talking to others who just got placed in jobs.** Often, individuals on serious job searches end up with more than one lead, which you can leverage to your benefit. These people are likely to have contacts for people who were looking to hire in the imminent future. Get these contacts if you can and follow up immediately. These are often the hottest leads you'll find.

That said, there are a few things that are almost certain to NOT work:

Do not send e-mail to the company's web site. This is the notorious HR black hole! In the words of one entertainment industry recruiter, "About half of the jobs I place come from internal referrals. Another 20 percent come from headhunters or professional placement agencies. I place about 5 to 10 percent of my jobs through resumes we received online or in the mail. The rest are people who we interviewed in the past but we didn't find a place for at the time"

So, e-mail sounds promising, right?

Not exactly – let's do the math: Every month there are about 10,000 new resumes received at these companies. In a given month, there may be 20 new positions. That means only 1-2 of the positions are filled through e-mail resumes. You have a one in 10,000 (or maybe a one in 5,000) chance of being picked in this manner. The longer it has been since the resume was sent, the lower the odds. Sending an e-mail cold is tough. While easier than winning the lotto, it is hardly encouraging enough to hinge your career upon. This is why so many resumes go into a black hole never to be heard from again.

That said, if you are going to send an e-mail because you have nothing else to lose, it costs no money and you have no other way of getting into the company or you're too lazy to figure it out, realize that many HR departments file resumes by how recently they were received. It may be a good idea to send multiple copies every few weeks, just to make sure that you are considered a 'recent' candidate.

Do not temp or work as an assistant thinking you'll "work your way up." While temping or serving as an assistant are THE paths (and often the only paths) into the creative side of the industry, the business side does not see administrative assistance as a training ground for the future leadership of a media conglomerate. One naïve graduate from a small college came to Los Angeles thinking that being an assistant would help him ascend to an analyst position. Only after a year in his role did he realize the move would be all but impossible. "I wish I'd known the truth so I wouldn't have given a year of my life to it," he now laments.

Build the right background. In looking for leads, remember this – you need to have the right background, not only in corporate jobs but business units as well. While experience is not necessary, positions such as strategy positions will be difficult to obtain without stellar performances in previous professional track positions like investment banks, consulting firms or other entertainment companies, or without the imprimatur of a top school or graduate program. Be realistic if you don't have these elements on your resume. There are many jobs in various media and entertainment companies. Find the ones that are the best fits with your background.

Our Survey Says: Lifestyle and Pay

Hours

Like so many industries, there is a work-life tradeoff that comes in the entertainment industry. "There are tons of tradeoffs," says one longtime employee in the strategic planning group of a studio. "The entertainment industry definitely doesn't come to mind when I think about a balanced lifestyle. It's a rare day I don't put in 12 hours."

But that's not always the case. There are many individuals that report (mostly outside of strategic planning and other corporate groups) consistently being home by 6. While the career trajectory is slower and the compensation is lower in the "business units" (versus the "corporate side"), the hours and the requirements are less demanding. There are always exceptions. Says one theme park executive: "Hours are usually 9 to 6, but every year for a few weeks in the spring during our five-year planning process, it's not uncommon for us to put in 12 hours a day, 7 days a week."

One rule of thumb: Corporate jobs that report to the CEO typically face "fire drills" (i.e. urgent deadlines imposed at the last minute) on a regular basis. Jobs that are more predictable (i.e., positions with business units rather than corporate-level positions) generally have more predictable hours.

Pay

"The pay in corporate jobs is usually up there with investment banking and management consulting," reports one former consultant-turned-analyst at a publishing house. The business units, however, are typically known for paying less, both because they are responsible for profit and loss (high salaries come straight out of the topline) and because of the less grueling hours. (For the difference between corporate and business units, see Organizational Chart of Media Companies.)

At the corporate level, beginning-level analysts out of college typically start at around $40,000, with several thousand dollars in bonus and a 15 percent raise after a year. Managers make at least $80,000 and directors usually crack six figures. VPs earn in the low $100k range.

In business units, the pay can be anywhere from 10 to 30 percent lower.

Other perks

Entertainment is attractive partly because of its perks. "Let's face it, I got into the industry hoping to hang out with rock stars," confesses one record industry insider. Employees get discounts on products, invitations to advance screenings of movies and tickets to movie premieres and gala parties. That said, the perks are not nearly as lavish as the expense accounts and freebies that come on the creative side of the business. There are the stories of the business folks who occasionally get free lunches, tickets to movie premieres and celebrity wedding invitations, but these are mostly the result of a person's personal connections.

Another practice, widely considered a perk, is that many within the industry itemize taxes and deduct all their entertainment expenses in the name of the job. "I itemized everything from my stereo to my movie tickets," boasts one corporate finance manager.

Promotions and competition

There is indeed jockeying for certain roles and positions, as there is in any industry, but the business side is not as ugly as the creative side when it comes to competition. Promotion decisions are not based on whether people like you, or on how your last film did, but rather on the body of your professional work. Even though there is an oversupply of people vying for the available jobs, it is a largely meritocratic industry.

Typical Career Path

Title	Responsibilities	Getting There
Phase 1 Analyst (Post-undergraduate positions often lasting 1-2 years)	Analyzing market data to understand new opportunities (e.g., roots of stagnation or decline, divestiture options, etc.) Creating countless Powerpoint presentations Responding to pressure-packed requests for data from executives	Personal and alumni networking Solicitations at management consulting and/or investment banks On-campus college recruiting
Phase 2 Manager/Director (Middle management, often post-MBA positions lasting 3-5 years)	Giving presentations and making recommendations Managing divisions or projects with profit and loss responsibility Creating business and operating plans for business units (e.g. home video, theme parks) Supervising market research and due diligence on prospective ventures	Recruiting out of MBA programs Internal corporate referrals
Phase 3 Vice President, Senior Vice President, Business Unit Head	Oversight of major business units (i.e. home video, consumer products) driving substantial parts of overall finances	Headhunters, executive search firms Promotions from within

The Interview

Typically, most interviews at the analyst level will be laid-back, candid discussions that walk a person through his or her resume and background. If there are many applicants or the interviewer is particularly anal, it will be more challenging. Your interest, passion and knowledge of the entertainment industry will prove particularly valuable.

Though everyone professes that no background is necessary, that is not entirely true. Often, interviewers will expect you to know the basics of the business model, the players and the major issues that confront a company. To find out what these are, it is best to read trade publications and analyst reports for the latest information. While subscriptions to these services may be expensive, it is often well worth the cost, especially if you are planning on having several interviews.

"The best ways to prep are to read trade publications, read analyst reports, get exposure to the industry, conduct informational interviews, use the products and of course, see a company's movies!" says one director-level strategic planning executive who has interviewed scores of candidates in his years in the industry. Additionally, it is useful to talk to every person you can who has been or is in a parallel position.

Beyond all this, the one thing to remember is this: you MUST believe in the work. Passion for the entertainment industry is impossible to fake because it is an industry where people live, breathe and sleep their jobs. If you're not one of those people, it shows.

Sample Questions and Answers

1. Explain [some technical term, i.e. exhibitor model].

This question that asks for specific industry knowledge is used to gauge whether you can hit the ground running. It is also used to estimate how well you did your homework. In some cases, it is an insanely technical question that a tough interviewer poses in search of the "perfect" candidate – in these cases, there is little that anyone can do to answer correctly. The best way to prepare is to talk to as many people in the industry as possible, read all current analyst reports (mostly available online for some fee), glance through the annual report to understand broad-scale initiatives, and conduct a literature search at a library to investigate if any articles have been written on the company's new business ventures.

2. Should we acquire [some company, i.e. Yahoo!]?

Since assessments of acquisitions are time-consuming, risky and largely the scope of big companies, such a question is not entirely uncommon. Usually it's tossed out only to finance jocks and consultants, but below is a general framework to answer the question:

- Discuss the products/services of the target company.

- Discuss the synergies with the company, or gaps in its product offering that could potentially be filled.

- Discuss a possible purchase price (a good estimate is its current market capitalization) and make an assessment as to whether the target is over- or undervalued.

The more you've read about the companies in question, the better you'll do.

3. Was our foray into [some business model, i.e. cruise ships] wise?

Entry into new businesses is another common question. Ask:

- Is the business itself a profitable one?

- Can your company now create efficiencies that did not exist before?

- Is there additional value that can be extracted from the venture, perhaps through a sale later on or through synergies with existing business divisions?

One bit of advice: if the venture was actually launched by the company you're interviewing with, it is almost always a good idea to support it, regardless of what really lies beneath the financials.

4. What do you think about [competitor's] decision to [make some acquisition]?

This is a slightly different spin on the acquisition question mentioned above. It requires a similar assessment of another company's acquisition. You need not be as positive in your assessment, however, as there is less of a risk that the interviewer maintains strong personal feelings about the acquisition.

5. Guess this weekend's box office pool.

Questions like this are tests to assess your passion for the industry. The entertainment industry is highly cyclical and extremely dependent on its release cycle – answer your question accordingly. For instance, if it is a weekend in the summer with a major picture being released, the weekend will be far larger than a weekend in April with nothing major coming out.

6. Why should we hire you over the 50 other people applying for this job?

While eagerness is good, experience is even better. If you have any relevant background that could make you particularly suited to the position you are seeking, now is the time to bring it up. Now is not the time to express humility. In the words of a former politician, "You are not great enough to be modest."

7. Give us some hard evidence that you're both interested in this position and that you are experienced enough to handle it.

It is best to think out a response to this question so you can present a cohesive and cogent answer. If you receive this question late in the interview, it's possible that your interviewer has tried to make this assessment of you based on your answers to prior interview questions, but is not persuaded yet.

Things To Watch Out For

You may have fought hard for your job offer, but there are some important questions you must ask before accepting The main features to look for in a job are:

Good managers. Are the managers good? Will they be respectful of your life outside of work? How do they manage their time and your own? Do they distribute work evenly, do they hoard good projects, do they let their subordinates shine?

Reasonable hours. What are the hours like? Is there face time? Are you expected to stay longer than your boss? Unless you ask directly, the hours may be longer than you think or than your interviewers represent.

Considerate lifestyle. Will you be working weekends? If so, how often? A company's response to this could be a deal breaker for you.

Reasonable promotions. What is the path to promotion? How does one ascend the corporate ladder? Does a set promotion happen after X months, or it is based on project flow? Is there a way that you can control your project flow – can you take on more work, or do different work if you want to?

Lots of growth. How is the company growing? Where is its future? Is it concentrated in one technology or strategy? Growth represents opportunities to shine and take the reins of new ventures.

Low turnover in the group. How many people have left in the past few years? How many people from three years ago are still in the group? Why do they leave and where do they go? This is a question that is best not posed to the person interviewing you, but the person you are replacing. High turnover should be a red flag.

Lateral movement opportunities. If you're interviewing in Theme Parks but really want to do Corporate Finance, how realistic is lateral movement? How long would you have to wait for that to happen? If no one's made the move in the past, you are unlikely to be the first to succeeed.

Flextime. Is telecommuting an option, or taking longer vacations? Will the worth of your team be questioned in an economic downturn? These are questions to gauge whether a company really wants you – they'll be more accommodating if you push them on this and they want you. If it's competitive and their budget is tight, they won't be very generous.

A promising future. Is this a high status or low status group? How insulated is it from the CEO? How integrated is it with the company's overall strategy? While the company may have a promising future, the specific position you take may have a different prognosis – make sure you understand the true story. If the product or business line is new, understand that poor performance may mean a pink slip.

Losing sleep over your job search?
Endlessly revising your resume?
Facing a work-related dilemma?

Super-charge your career with Vault's newest career tools: Resume Reviews, Resume Writing, and Career Coaching.

Vault Resume Writing

On average, a hiring manager weeds through 120 resumes for a single job opening. Let our experts write your resume from scratch to make sure it stands out.

- Start with an e-mailed history and 1- to 2-hour phone discussion
- Vault experts will create a first draft
- After feedback and discussion, Vault experts will deliver a final draft, ready for submission

Vault Resume Review

- Submit your resume online
- Receive an in-depth e-mailed critique with suggestions on revisions within TWO BUSINESS DAYS

Vault Career Coach

Whether you are facing a major career change or dealing with a workplace dilemma, our experts can help you make the most educated decision via telephone counseling sessions.

- Sessions are 45 minutes over the telephone

"I have rewritten this resume 12 times and in one review you got to the essence of what I wanted to say!"

– S.G. Atlanta, GA

"It was well worth the price! I have been struggling with this for weeks and in 48 hours you had given me the answers! I now know what I need to change."

– T.H. Pasadena, CA

"I found the coaching so helpful I made three appointments!"

– S.B. New York, NY

For more information go to www.vault.com/careercoach

VAULT
> the insider career network™

The Creative Side: Hiring

CHAPTER 6

Breaking In

Background and preparation

There is very little formal background that one needs to acquire a position in the creative side of the entertainment industry. The frequency with which people are replaced is a testament to the replaceability of most jobs in the industry.

The job requirements are surprisingly generic. As in other industries, entertainment companies seek individuals who are hardworking, passionate, charismatic, intelligent and honest.

The hardest part of getting hired on the creative side is knowing where to look. There is no formal recruiting or training program, there are no job fairs, formal ads are rare and news often travels by word of mouth. You have to work hard, smile even (and especially) when you're down, keep looking when doors are closed, hold your head up high when humiliated. Even then, there is the elusive factor of luck in meeting the right person at the right time that you'll need to get anywhere.

"Without a network, it can be scary. Lots of young starlets come to New York or Los Angeles and leave soon after. Others end up sticking it out because they have no other choice. They used the only savings they had to come out here in the first place," says one Hollywood TV writer who came to the industry over a decade ago.

The best ways to get a foot in the door are to:

Take classes. Numerous classes abound throughout the industry – screenwriting, novel writing, acting, producing. UCLA and NYU have extension school classes which are great for networking with other up-and-comers in the industry. Just as important as classmates are professors, who often have some contacts within the industry. For years, UCLA offered a class in its extension school called Screenwriters on Screenwriting, which provided exposure to Hollywood's top writers. Not only was the class a prime opportunity to meet individuals who had "made it," but it also provided inspiration for aspiring artists. Classes like these are wonderful for both fueling creative juices and cultivating contacts throughout town.

Temp. There are some entertainment-specific temp agencies, known for placing people in positions in studios or at entertainment companies. Try to find them and get in the door. Some of them will only take you with a

---

The Competition

As in the business side, there are numerous stereotypes that abound. The classic characters include:

The Eager Beaver – Fresh Hollywood arrivals, often in their first jobs, extremely eager to please.

The Cutthroat – Highly competitive types on a pernicious mission to be promoted; often former Eager Beavers.

The Mid-Careerists – Older (i.e. thirtysomething) arrivals embarking upon a career in entertainment for the first time.

The Angeleno/New Yorker – Lifelong residents of the media capitals who landed in their positions because it was their first job.

The Aspiring Artist – True creatives paying their bills with a day job but looking for a place to send their manuscripts and demo tapes.

---

referral, but persistence is often the key to getting in. Unlike business jobs where there is an impenetrable rift between professionals and their support staff, a temp position in a creative job could actually land you a full time position.

Intern for free. While not the most appealing track because it is so unattractive (menial labor for no pay), interning can provide you the credibility you need to land a job elsewhere. Make a list of everyone you know and want to target. Write to them. Ask them if there's anything you can do. Ask other interns if they had a good experience. It's always easier to follow in the footsteps of someone who has blazed the path. This is where the cold-calling and faxing into the ether may not be bad. One young aspiring filmmaker landed a job by sending e-mails to over 75 people, and then following up. "Most people didn't even bother responding to me, but one person at a TV studio just happened to be looking for a PA when I inquired. I started work the next Monday."

Buy *The Hollywood Creative Directory*. While expensive for a book (approximately $60) and voluminous (there are several versions), it is a gold mine. "Go get it – NOW," advises one creative executive. Within it are all the names, addresses and phone numbers you'll need to make your initial contacts. Getting to know the names within will familiarize you with the industry, inform your reading of the trades, could score you an internship and give you contacts that could provide a referral or two.

Do at least 10 informational interviews. Leverage alumni networks. Strike up conversations at bars. Go to any conferences or speaker engagements you can find. Get business cards and follow up. Ask people for referrals for informational interviews. In fact, there are many universities that are known for being particularly strong within entertainment – Northwestern, Harvard, Stanford, UCLA, USC, NYU, University of Florida and others. Even if you didn't attend one of these schools, meeting people who did may provide you an entry point into their networks through mixers, parties and other social events.

Offer to contribute script coverage. While many script reading jobs are unionized positions and not easy to find, it can be a way to break in. Sometimes, if a person really likes you but wasn't able to hire you, you should ask if you can do some coverage to make a little money on the side. That said, keep in mind that script coverage does not pay tons of money – scripts typically pay about $50 each.

Get into an agency. Talent agencies, while brutal, have lines of job seekers not unlike the DMV. If you are lucky to eventually get an interview once you fill out an employment application, you may be given the opportunity to start in the mail room. Take the job. It is both an entry point as well as a way to meet people that you may not have exposure to otherwise. Often the human resources group can be found by calling information and having them direct you (believe us, you won't be the first) or by simply showing up with your resume, being directed to the office and filling out an application form. Of course, an appointment is always best, but if you look groomed, persistent and promising, they may ask you to come back for an interview.

Leverage your alumni network. This is one of the most important resources you can use. Schools often have lists of many alumni in a given industry. Ask your alumni office for a copy. When you meet people, take them to coffee or lunch. Try to find out as much as you can about a person beforehand – that makes conversation easier, and it's easier these days with the Internet. Get to the point, and ask them if there's anyone else they can recommend, or if they would mind you getting in touch with them or someone in their office soon. Whenever you follow up, always have something interesting to say about some new lead that you've found – there's nothing more annoying than people who keep pestering a few contacts for a job without any indication that they're making things happen for themselves.

Leverage any network you can. Make friends who may have access to information. Prod people about what they're doing, where they came from, if there's anyone you could talk to. The industry still circulates the acclaimed and notorious UTA job list, which originated from the United Talent Agency, one of Hollywood's biggest agencies. The best way to find this list is by befriending someone who works at a talent agency.

Know the trades. Pore over the trade periodicals (*Hollywood Reporter*, *Variety*, *Billboard*, *Publishers Weekly*, to a lesser degree *Premiere* and *Movieline*) to get a sense of all the key players in the field you're interested in. Know the trades inside and out so that you are on top of what movies get made, what TV projects are in development, who the hot new music acts are, what manuscripts are in play at the top publishing houses and, most of all, if there are any openings that mean opportunities for you.

Go to film school. While an expensive endeavor and a difficult one (acceptance rates are often in the single digits for programs like the American Film Institute, NYU Film School, UCLA Film School, and USC School of Cinema & Television), film school can provide valuable contacts, not only in the form of an alumni network, on-campus speakers and job-hunting, but also in the form of companionship with dozens of classmates all entering the creative industry with aspirations of fame and fortune. While full-time film school programs are often the most rewarding, there are also numerous smaller, less expensive programs, which may not lend much in the way of credibility, but will likely help you create a reel, demo tape or portfolio.

Our Survey Says: Lifestyle and Pay

Hours

The hours on the creative side, especially at the assistant level, are brutal. Long, backbreaking hours for little pay and often questionable reward are the norm. It is an unspoken rule of the junior ranks that one must arrive every morning before one's manager and stay at least until they leave. The hours drive many people to flee from the industry within a year of their arrival. After being promoted beyond assistant, however, the hours become more flexible. Even so, there is often the implicit pressure of savage competition, making it essential to put in plenty of facetime.

Family

Flexibility to have children or time for them is very difficult to find. As you move up the ladder, you will be able to exert more control over your schedule and work hours. Still, spending time mingling and schmoozing is vital, since many promotions and deals hinge on personal relationships. It is difficult to not feel left out in the cold when everyone else is at an industry function on weekends or weekdays.

Pay

Assistants make between $500 and $900 a week, depending on the job. Agent assistants and production assistants usually make $500, while assistants for studio executives and producers make closer to the higher end of this range (both because overtime is built in and studios have labor laws that force them to treat hourly workers with more respect). From the assistant position, creative types usually make the leap to a "manager" level position. It is a big deal to make the leap out of the assistant position, though the ascension is more a matter of title and responsibilities than compensation. While the specific titles vary, the overall job description is largely the same. Annual incomes for the story editor/manager/director of development position is between $40k – $60k, but it is a salary (you're off the punch-in clock) and you get an expense account for meals (a big deal!), not to mention a cell phone.

The VP title pays in the $60k – $125k range, depending upon the company, your experience and your negotiation skills. In general, studios usually pay more than production companies unless the production company has a lot of projects going on (or if you bring in a lot of projects). In that case, you will be compensated similarly to how you would be paid at a studio. You might get a bonus for setting up projects, a production fee if/when a project gets made and a low-level producer credit once it is executed. Agents usually make a guaranteed base and then get a cut of the commissions they book. In the smaller agencies, you're expected to earn back your base first, and then you get a cut. Good agents make quite a bit of money because their salary is entirely contingent upon the deals that they execute. Less ambitious or successful agents naturally make less. Typically the starting salary for an agent is $40k-50k.

Studio executives get higher salaries because they don't get any bonuses or commissions. In studios, the "big money" occurs when you work your way up the VP ladder at the studio (executive vice president, senior vice president, etc.).

Other perks

The perks of the entertainment profession are many and enticing. There are the lavish premieres, the tickets to special parties, the exposure to celebrities, the generous expense accounts and, of course, the involvement in creating pop culture. Beyond the glamour of the industry, there are other more pragmatic advantages, such as company cars from some jobs and even subsidized home loans. Beyond the schmoozing, one of the most popular perks of working in the industry is the tax benefit. Many who work in the entertainment industry save money by writing off all entertainment expenses (e.g. movie tickets, stereo equipment, magazines) as itemized elements on the IRS Schedule B.

Promotions and competition

The industry is tough. In fact, it can be downright brutal. There are many people vying for a few positions. The biggest downside of the creative side of entertainment is the lack of job security. "You get fired all the time," are the words of one TV producer. Take a quick look through one of Hollywood's big trade periodicals and it quickly becomes clear that people are constantly changing jobs. The entire industry, in fact, is one big perpetual game of musical chairs.

Even though the industry is tough, often with long, draining, grueling hours that chip away at one's ego and self-esteem, it's not impossible. You will be rewarded for delivering a great movie, a blockbuster book or a hit record, and you can often ride on the coattails of others who do. And you only need one or two big hits to make it for life.

Everyone starts on the bottom rung. Even if you have a JD or an MBA, you'll still need to start out opening fan mail or getting coffee. Keep networking and keep smiling.

Typical Career Path

	Title	Responsibilities	Getting There
Phase 0	Internship (Unpaid positions that are starting points for making contacts)	Xeroxing, running errands, filing Writing script coverage of incoming screenplays Answering phones	Cold calling production companies or producers Sending cover letters and following up
Phase 1	Creative/Production Assistant (Low-paying positions that last at least one year, often several)	Handling your managers' phone calls Writing script coverage of incoming screenplays Keeping abreast of "hot talent" being picked up by other studios, agencies and production companies Some personal errands (e.g. dry-cleaning, picking up kids from school, kitchen cleaning, fridge stocking)	Personal and alumni networking Informational interviews Making friends with other assistants
Phase 2	Manager/Director of Development or Production	Reviewing scripts/talent from agents (or sending them out if you are an agent) Pitching (with writers) concepts/stories to studios to get "green lit" Keeping up with trends or new developments that could help get you more work	Networking and waiting for an opening Reading trade publications like *Variety* or *Hollywood Reporter* for changes of the guard
Phase 3	Vice President, President, Multi-Picture Deals	The ability to green light pictures and push along things that interest you	Networking Promotions from within

The Interview

If you can get a formal job interview for a creative position, you will have achieved an accomplishment where many others have failed. Rarely are interviews on the creative side challenging from an intellectual standpoint. More often than not, questions are general inquiries about your background, why you want to be in entertainment, if you understand the job description, etc. In fact, the most challenging aspect is the inevitable behavioral tests, in which interviewers do everything from keeping a job aspirant waiting for hours, to talking to a prospective candidate while they are getting their hair done. The creative side of entertainment is, after all, mostly about finding the right "fit" for people.

There is a small, small chance that a person will face really tough or outright hostile questions. If that happens, they are often similar to these questions that follow. Below are also some suggestions given by aspiring creative types who have landed recent positions:

Sample Questions and Answers

1. What network do you bring to the table?

Naturally, the key hiring criteria for any creative type is what they will be able to contribute to a production roster. The wider the network, the wealthier the network, the more integrated the network into the industry, the better. Most respondents should talk about their college networks, and any industry stars they have encountered.

2. What writers/actors/talent do you know personally?

This is an answer that is difficult to bluff and often takes years within the industry to answer well. It is also the single biggest determinant of who is a "player."

3. Do you have examples of coverage?

"Coverage" is basically a summary of a spec script that has been submitted to a production company or a talent agency with a recommendation as to whether or not it is worthy of further consideration. The format of coverage varies from company to company, but it is best to have "coverage" in your back pocket prior to a film interview. The best way to do this is to befriend a media assistant who will be able to give you access to a new script about which you should compose your sample of coverage.

4. What's your creative sensibility?

This is a softball question to answer because it requires no background other than really knowing yourself. If asked this question at the beginning of an interview, it is a test to see if you fit. If asked at the end, it is usually a courtesy question. Have an answer prepared. Conviction is most important.

5. Don't you think you're overqualified for this position?

This is a common question with an agenda. It posed is to separate the wheat from the proverbial chaff. One must almost by definition start as an assistant of some sort in the entertainment industry, regardless of background. So the issue of qualification is really moot – there is no such thing as overqualification. The best way to answer this question is to acknowledge that truism and emphasize your willingness to work hard.

Things To Watch Out For

First and foremost, in the creative industry, you want to look for anyone willing to hire you, which in itself can be a daunting and exhausting task. Once that has occurred, you can get a sense of the the career opportunities ahead:

- Why did the person who preceded you leave?

- What resources do you have to make things happen in the industry?

- Will those resources be shared?

- Are the expectations for the position clear? What will be your day-to-day duties?

- Does the company promote from within?

- Where have previous employees gone? Have they been driven out of the profession entirely, or do they typically end up better off?

- Will you get regular reviews of your performance?

- Ask yourself if you liked your interviewer. Remember that personality is key.

Use the Internet's
MOST TARGETED
job search tools.

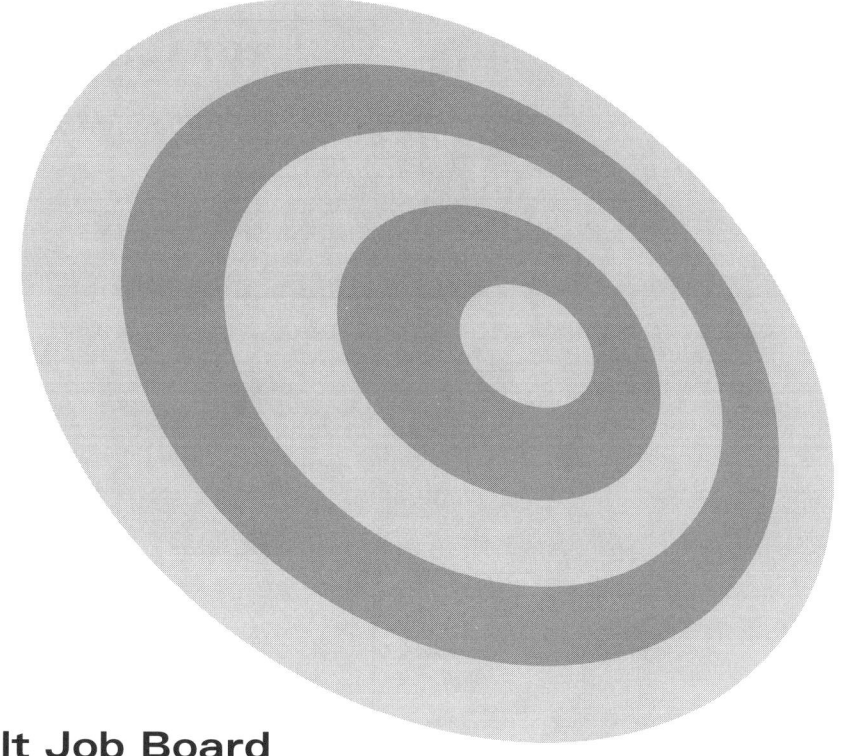

Vault Job Board

Target your search by industry, function, and experience level, and find the job openings that you want.

VaultMatch Resume Database

Vault takes match-making to the next level: post your resume and customize your search by industry, function, experience and more. We'll match job listings with your interests and criteria and e-mail them directly to your inbox.

V/\ULT
> the insider career network™

VAULT CAREER GUIDES
GET THE INSIDE SCOOP ON TOP JOBS

"Cliffs Notes for Careers"
– *FORBES MAGAZINE*

Vault guides and employer profiles have been published since 1997 and are the premier source of insider information on careers.

Each year, Vault surveys and interviews thousands of employees to give readers the inside scoop on industries and specific employers to help them get the jobs they want.

"To get the unvarnished scoop, check out Vault"
– *SMARTMONEY MAGAZINE*

VAULT

ON THE JOB

Chapter 7: The Business Side: The Jobs

Chapter 8: The Creative Side: The Jobs

Chapter 9: Survival Skills for Assistants

Chapter 10: Dream Jobs

The Business Side: The Jobs

CHAPTER 7

The business side of entertainment is about everything except creation of content. This chapter is about all the behind-the-scenes work that ends up in the pages of *BusinessWeek*, *The Wall Street Journal* and *Fortune* – the mergers and acquisitions that allow companies to grow, the market research that says "yes" to a launch of a new company initiative or the business plan outlining the growth of an existing asset. These are the divisions of the company that determine the higher-level strategic decisions that form the backbone of a media company, determine its market capitalization, affect the bulk of its share price and ultimately drive overall revenue and profitability.

Within the business side, there are three groups: 1) the corporate-level groups that involve very high-level business decisions that have a large impact on the company's bottom line, 2) the divisions (a.k.a. business units) that work in the trenches of a specific operation with an immediate impact on revenues, profits and losses and 3) the standard overarching business functions evident in every company (e.g. accounting, legal, human resources, IT).

15 Popular Job Tracks

Corporate Level Positions

Strategic planning
Strategic planning groups are small groups of about five to 40 professionals that serve as in-house consulting and investment banking arms. Not coincidentally, most employees are ex-consultants and bankers. Strategists are involved in valuation and negotiation decisions for acquisitions, business plans for new ventures, the expansion of the current business lines (and sometimes creating new ones), forward-looking financial plans to provide budgeting and overall prognosis for the health of all divisions of the company, and any other high-level issues that the company as a whole may be facing.

Because these projects affect the overall health of the company, meetings are often power sessions in the corporate dining room or top-floor board rooms with the company's senior executives, including the CEO, COO and CFO. While exposure to these individuals is one of the perks of this position, the jobs also tend to be incredibly challenging and taxing, as inordinate amounts of background data, research and information are synthesized and spun into a story prior to the presentation of findings. This group's job is all the more challenging, given that the recommendations that strategic planning groups deliver must necessarily be at odds with decisions that have already been made. Strategic planners, after all, are constantly trying to maximize the returns on the company's capital, which means analyzing and dismissing many current projects.

This function is also sometimes called corporate development, business development or in-house consulting. Because of the frequent exposure to high-level executives, the overall clout of the group and its impact in the major decisions of media conglomerates, these tend to be highly sought-after jobs, mostly filled by top-notch MBAs.

Corporate finance

Corporate finance is a sister group to strategic planning. Corporate financiers are the people who work in concert with investment bankers (or in lieu of them) to price deals, investigate options and plot the course of the company's growth through acquisitions of other companies.

Nearly all the major entertainment companies have grown through major acquisitions in the past two decades, increasing the importance of their corporate financiers. Corporate finance professionals investigate acquisition opportunities, gather competitive intelligence on other companies, determine synergies and negotiate deals. Likewise, they also divest businesses that may be undesirable in exchange for cash.

Most individuals in the corporate finance function are former investment bankers, accounting wizards and CFOs-to-be who bring their expertise in finance and public company performance to the entertainment industry.

Case Study: Publishing Industry, Magazine Strategy

Company: Conde Nast

Division: Strategic Marketing

Project: Investigate opportunities to bundle magazine subscriptions

Conde Nast, the parent company of many of the country's most popular magazines, *Vogue, GQ, The New Yorker, Vanity Fair* and others, was facing some issues, such as diminishing subscription numbers, lower advertising revenues and loss of market share to competitive offerings on the Internet. The question was how to increase distribution and sell-through of magazines within its family. One solution proposed by a senior executive was to bundle various titles together into packages.

A corporate strategic planning executive was given the task of determining the efficacy and profitability of such a venture. The initial step was to meet with the circulation department and get numbers on what the current subscriptions were, and to see how large the numbers could potentially be.

The steps that the executive took were as follows:

- Talk to the direct marketing and market research teams to understand who the current customers were

- Learn about their current behavior

- Assess any opportunity to provide bundles

- Estimate the cost of implementing a marketing campaign that would present the option to readers

In the end, it was determined that the cost of providing new bundles would require millions more dollars of marketing spending and would involve a degree of operational complexity that would prevent such a program from being worthwhile. However, a finding from the research that did make sense was that increased cross-selling and leveraging of the company's existing database – something surprisingly underutilized – would be far more practical.

This new project, cross-selling within the database, ended up delivering a significant increase in the number of subscribers to the company's flagship magazines, nearly double that of some prior marketing efforts.

Corporate marketing

Corporate marketing assesses consumer reaction to new projects, initiatives and endeavors. Often these groups are direct reports of business units (where each division has its own marketing group), but there are also many cases in which these groups are centralized under corporate and provide their services on an as-needed basis. The benefit of centralized marketing is that it enables the sharing of data across the company since the information is compiled by one group that can then spread the information. It also provides leverage with outside vendors (advertising agencies, media placement agencies, market research firms) when negotiating fees: the more money a company plans on spending with one deal, the better its negotiating position when choosing among competing agencies.

Corporate marketing encompasses many objectives:

- Market research and the execution of both quantitative and qualitative research

- The management of outside vendors who oversee new software, focus groups or large research studies

- Determining revenue projections for new products

- Soliciting consumer feedback on new and existing products

- Creating pricing models

- Estimating market penetration and rollout strategies

- Authoring marketing plans

- Supervising advertising and direct mail

- Overseeing overall brand equity and elements of brand differentiation like logo and identity

- Overseeing product-specific public relations efforts that drive coverage in the media

Corporate marketers often have an extensive background with advertising agencies or marketing consultancy firms.

Corporate public relations

For years, corporate PR was considered to be exclusively for damage control during events like the Exxon Valdez or the Tylenol cyanide scare. Whenever a CEO had problems with the press,, the white knights of corporate PR came to the rescue to help avert a worse catastrophe. Corporate PR groups still perform this function. However, the work of corporate PR groups is much broader than just handling crisis management. Corporate PR groups now manage corporate spokespersons, serve as experts on media training and public appearances and coach CEOs as they prepare for media appearances and event marketing.

The corporate PR group is also known for initiating major press coverage in industry and business trade publications, as well as corporate-focused articles in general interest magazines like *Time, Newsweek* or *Vanity Fair*. PR professionals also develop relationships with government officials and lobbying groups that may have influence over legislation affecting the company's growth and development. Often, this group works with outside public relations agencies like Edelman Worldwide, Bozell or Hill & Knowlton.

Internet strategy
As content becomes increasingly commoditized due to the fact that so much on the Internet is free, there are challenges in protecting the hallowed material that entertainment companies create. While studios would love to use the Internet to hoard their content and prevent anyone else from distributing and profiting from it (sort of a preemptive strike against companies like Napster), the Internet is also an incredibly seductive resource for marketing, mainly because information can be communicated broadly and cheaply – much more inexpensively than TV commercials, billboards and bus shelters. The popularity of *The Blair Witch Project*, a surprise hit, was partially attributed to a very effective web site.

This tension (to promote our properties or protect them?) feeds the very complex and critical role that Internet strategy plays in the growth of media and entertainment companies. Because of the constantly evolving and still uncertain nature of the business, there are hundreds of individuals at nearly all major entertainment companies, tracking evolving technologies, coding pages, maintaining fresh web site content and otherwise marketing via the Web. Media companies with Internet strategy groups include Walt Disney/ABC and AOL Time Warner.

Real estate development
Real estate development within an entertainment company involves not only theme parks, but also extensions of an entertainment empire's brands, including themed restaurants (Hard Rock Café), sports stadiums, entertainment complexes (Sony Metreon) and other destinations that involve large tracts of land that can both provide steady revenue streams and impress an entertainment-seeking audience. The major entertainment companies

often have proprietary lots of their own land that were either part of the company's origin (as Disney does with its land in Florida and Southern California, now managed under the aegis of the Disney Development Corporation), were results of acquisitions or were acquired over time.

As real estate development is its own unique business with special financing rules and its own intrinsic rewards, the field generally attracts individuals from outside the entertainment industry. The most successful individuals in these divisions are those with substantial experience managing vendors, contractors and landscape architects, working with community development offices, leveraging tax benefits and executing visionary blueprints. Real estate development is a particularly exciting division for individuals wishing to combine interests in the hospitality industry, finance and real estate.

Business Unit Positions

Home video management

Home video is a multi-billion dollar business and arguably the most critical component of a film's revenue stream. Even the biggest blockbusters are often not profitable until this phase of the film's life cycle, meaning that the difference between a red or black bottom line often boils down to what happens with home video distribution and marketing.

Much home video business comes from video stores like Blockbuster and Hollywood Video that pay top dollar for copies of releases, but a substantial part also comes directly from consumers in retail channels like Wal-Mart and Costco (also called sell-through or "DTC," direct-to-consumer). The value of a movie property in home video can generally be predicted based on its prior box office performance, though sometimes a movie performs modestly at the box office but becomes a hit on video. For most titles, there are established routines and marketing plans accompanying releases (video stores first, then release to retail stores, sometimes with a marketing campaign and in-store promotions to support it). The biggest departments in this group tend to be in finance and in operations/distribution. One feature unique to home video is that relatively little money is allocated to promoting properties that are unproven. Proven films often tend to promote themselves. Because of this, marketing tends to be less important than at film studios.

Once exception to this rule is Disney, which has a more robust creative and marketing group in its home video division, due to the vast number of animated properties it owns and some unique features in its business strategy. First, Disney has a seven-year release cycle for animated classics such as

Snow White and *Dumbo*. To this end, large promotional campaigns in print, TV and in-store must supplement each release to catch the attention of the latest crop of kids. In the interim years, Disney boosts sales by releasing several DTV (direct-to-video) movies such as *Simba's Pride* or *Aristocats 2*, all of which also need supplementary promotion, usually in the form of inexpensive in-store, Sunday circular or McDonald's marketing. Much of the creative production of these DTVs happens in-house. (This actually serves as an inroad into the creative process for some aspiring filmmakers.)

Home video finance groups often create Excel models that predict sales to stores and pinpoint the most effective distribution outlets. With the shift from VHS to DVD, there are also substantial efforts in home video divisions everywhere to assess the cost and gain of this change.

Operations and distribution managers deal specifically with retail chains, working out high-volume deals that encourage stores to carry more of a studio's films, to place them prominently within a store and to make sure that those stocks don't run out (in retail, called a "stock-out"). Marketing managers create physical in-store promotions and orchestrate marketing strategies that would drive consumers to buy the video (e.g., a promotion with a fast food restaurant, coupons in newspapers, direct mail, infomercials, etc.)

While often viewed as unsexy because it is far removed from the creative process, home video has spawned many stars in the ranks of media companies because of its solid revenue stream and ability to generate surefire profits for the bottom line of major media companies. The prognosis for the industry is optimistic, with the industry shift to DVD encouraging people to amass new movie collections. Video-on-demand (VOD) is sometimes cited as a threat to the home video industry, but with studios slow to move and regulatory hurdles involving bandwidth still unresolved, the home video business will likely be around for a while. That said, the international market for VOD is virtually nil, which still leaves a nice, fat revenue stream for home video no matter what.

Consumer products licensing

While not all companies have the appropriate media properties to capitalize on a consumer products division, many make producing consumer goods a substantial part of their business strategy. All the Mickey beach towels, Daffy toothbrush holders and *Blue's Clue's* bedsheets that make their ways to Wal-Mart and Target are there thanks to the ambition and shrewd negotiating talents of some of media's smartest business executives. "This is the mother lode of the entire business," says one Warner Brothers executive in charge of the company's Harry Potter licensing program.

Consumer products divisions are often divided into two groups. The first is the licensing business; the second is retail (see next section). Licensing brings loads of cash straight to the company's coffers, with little to no overhead. Manufacturers of just about anything in the world, from cell phones to children's clothes to crayons, pay money (in deals that often last many years) to have the exclusive rights to use images of Porky Pig or Donald Duck on their products. Though generally a lucrative division, many media companies enter the consumer products business only to realize that it is very difficult to execute well – licensees are often discriminating and there is always the risk of brand dilution for the licensor. Even Disney, widely regarded as the big kahuna of consumer products licensing, faltered in the late 1990s with the overextension of its licensing business.

Consumer products licensing can be a tough business. The plus side is that with a lucrative property it can be cash cow, putting the managers of the licensing businesses in the unique position of being able to call the shots with other senior executives and often with vendors, an enviable position in an entertainment company.

Retail stores development

Another aspect of the licensing business is the retail operation – the stores that carry branded products and are operated by the company. Examples are The Disney Stores, The Warner Brothers Studio Stores and more recently, the Nickelodeon Stores. While not as successful or profitable as the licensing business due to high overhead costs (and a weak retail environment overall), they are generally solid contributors to corporate brand equity and are training grounds for senior executives by providing critical exposure to customers, consumer marketing and research, finance, operations and real estate. In addition to the traditional store part of retail, this division also is entrusted with direct mail, online stores and any sales of proprietary merchandise.

The retail side offers exposure to running a business. That said, with even Disney shutting down some of its stores, the retail business will likely not be a driver for growth, making it a nice place to learn, but not to stay.

Theme parks management

While not all the major entertainment companies have theme parks to promote their filmed properties, many of the major ones do, and within these divisions lie some intriguing business opportunities. In the beginning, it was just pretty much Disneyland and Disney World and some regional players in between, but in the last 15 years, there has been a big push within other major entertainment companies, primarily Universal Studios and Paramount (through the acquisition of Great America) to round out their leisure portfolios.

Like the consumer products division, theme parks, attractions and resorts are an enormously important part of an entertainment empire's business as they are both tremendous capital investments and a reliable source of revenue. Driving consumers to the park and keeping them coming back for more is key to making a park profitable. Entrance fees to parks are often hefty, averaging about $30 per day per customer (with additional money spent on food and gifts). Companies like average stays to last at least several hours. In the case of the domestic Disney theme parks, that average is several days.

For that reason, marketing plays a very important role. Companies like Disney and Universal believe creating an unforgettable experience captures lifelong customers who may be loyal to other products the company creates. The best ways to drive people there are with discounts, promotions, special offers and tailored marketing campaigns to high-spending subgroups such as business conventions, trade shows and weddings. All this translates into robust marketing opportunities at theme parks.

Another interesting trend in the theme park world is the growing trend toward licensing. In this case, the daily operation of the theme park, the real estate costs and buildout are financed by another company, but the name and marketing are the responsibility of the licensing company. This allows a company to capture substantial revenues without incurring capital expenditures. Disney does this with a theme park in Japan and has been exploring this option in other venues as well.

Theme park management is an exciting business with a promising future due to growth (new parks being built by Universal and Disney) and a small landscape of competitors (e.g. Club Med, cruise ships). That said, there are numerous opportunities in marketing, finance and operations, all of which are exciting because of their practical, hands-on roles and their contribution to overall corporate revenue. (One key factor to keep in mind is the geographic location of theme parks – they are often located on the periphery of large metropolises such as Anaheim, CA and Orlando, FL, or in Europe, outside of Barcelona and Paris.)

Case Study: Real Estate Development/Themed Entertainment

Company: The Walt Disney Company
Division: Disney Regional Entertainment
Project: Investigate the extension of a new location-based entertainment (LBE) venture.

The Walt Disney Company is one of the world's largest media and entertainment conglomerates, with involvement in motion pictures and filmed entertainment, retail and theme parks.

In the late 1980s and early 1990s, Disney wanted to investigate opportunities beyond Orlando and Anaheim (the homes of its major theme parks), and create an entertainment franchise that attracted an older age group than children attracted to theme parks. Given advances in technology and findings from market research, it seemed that the video game industry was a good one to tackle. Disney began to look at video games and similar forms of entertainment that could be recreated in a smaller arcade-like setting.

The key steps in executing the project were coordinating with Imagineers (Disney's engineering team) to create concepts for the proposed project and conducting market research to test the feasibility of the venture. The result of these first two phases of work was the creation of DisneyQuest, essentially a Disney-themed arcade. The first DisneyQuest was launched in Orlando at the company's Magic Kingdom. Once the division proved that it had "legs" and that it could potentially survive as a freestanding location in another city, the next step was to do a location analysis to determine what the most profitable and receptive venues for the Disney brand in other parts of the United States would be. After some time, DisneyQuest was also launched in Chicago.

Disney's Chicago venue eventually proved to be unsuccessful (it was closed in 2001), due more to the company's pulling back from broader location-based-entertainment ventures than poor attendance. Executives at the company felt it was best to focus on the core businesses, which in fact were now facing the crunch of an economic downturn. That said, the company decided to keep the venue in Orlando, which it continues to operate successfully.

Film distribution and theater management

Distribution involves the dissemination of films both within the United States and to international markets. Within the U.S., films are distributed to theater chains, which purchase copies of a film to show. Movie theaters generally make little to no money on the actual airing of the film, especially during the first few weekends of a film's release. While they do make some revenue if the film plays for many weeks, in general, their revenues come primarily from food, beverages, arcades and other concessions. Major theater chains are often located outside of Los Angeles and New York. Regal Theaters, the country's largest chain, is headquartered in Tennessee.

The international market is more fragmented than the U.S. market. International distribution typically involves partnerships with foreign import-export firms, who then make deals in their respective markets to translate and distribute films to local theaters. Global distribution often tends to be tricky, as international film markets are loaded with unique and quirky rules (e.g., no onscreen kissing or other sexual activity in certain markets) and regulatory groups (often monopolies dominated by individuals who make up their own rules) that may require some additional editing of the film for a particular market.

Television distribution works in a similar manner, but instead of theater chains, entertainment companies deal with other television networks in foreign markets.

Case Study: Television, Strategic Planning

Company: Fox Family Channel
Division: Children's Programming
Project: To formulate a plan to increase Fox's ratings in children's daytime programming

Twentieth Century Fox was one of the early pioneers of the film industry. After its acquisition by Rupert Murdoch's News Corp, the Fox brand was expanded into other areas of entertainment, including television. As Fox established the U.S.'s fourth major network, executive management expanded into other areas of programming as well – namely sports and children's television.

The Fox Family Channel was created primarily to provide an alternative to Nickelodeon. Similar to Nickelodeon, Fox was known for edgy, more "fluffy" programming that, while aimed at children 8-13, actually attracted younger children. One of the key timeslots when children's programming had to succeed was Saturday morning – the children's programming equivalent of Thursday evening primetime.

For several seasons, Fox's Saturday morning cartoon lineup had been characterized by low ratings and reviewers who felt the content was "immature and stale." The characters on Fox TV shows were also associated with low Q-scores (the entertainment industry ranking of popular characters, usually a factor of awareness and how much children like them).

A SWAT team of strategic planners was then called in to assess the situation. Why weren't the Fox shows working? What on other TV networks was working? In general, when did children watch television? What type of programming resonated with children? What did kids these days find cool? Focus groups and one-on-one interviews were conducted with young children, school teachers and parents throughout the country to analyze Fox's performance and overall brand equity among this demographic. The findings were then relayed to a programming/creative team entrusted with creating new concepts that would "wow" children everywhere.

Due to the mammoth task of creating and repositioning a programming schedule, senior executives at the company grew to be impatient with the continued sagging ratings and declining advertising revenue. Just as new shows were being pitched and piloted, Fox sold its network to Disney, which rebranded the network as ABC Family.

Other Entry Points into Entertainment: General Overarching Functions

While these positions are not nearly as sexy as others, they are important and can often be a launching pad into other areas of the industry. Furthermore, they require little previous background in the media and entertainment industry.

Accounting

As in any company, accounting often forms a critical part of the business, especially in larger public companies. The media and entertainment industry is no exception, where the often murky costs of creative talent and entertainment financing further complicate issues and increase demand for talented CPAs and professionals who are versed in accounting rules and the degree of compliance that they necessitate.

Human resources

Like accounting, this is also a substantial and critical part of a company, integrating many of the typical things that HR departments oversee, like benefits, compensation and employee protection.

Information technology

Integrating new and revolutionary technologies, databases, market research findings and different, intricate accounting metrics is always an enormous task, and the decentralized divisions in an entertainment company, as in any other company, make such projects long and time-consuming. Media IT groups, therefore, retain even larger budgets and have many of the largest IT consulting firms on retainer in their attempts to bring their companies into the latest information-sharing age.

Legal

The legal function is particularly critical in the media and entertainment industry. There are lots of intellectual property protection issues, trademark and copyright infringement issues and lawsuits filed by individuals who feel they have been wronged by a studio or company that has "stolen work." As media and entertainment is also a human-intensive business with many transactions based on deals between people, it is only natural that there are legal protections in place to assure that they are properly conducted. The business affairs departments of Hollywood studios are almost exclusively made up of law school graduates and former attorneys.

Organizational Chart of Media Companies

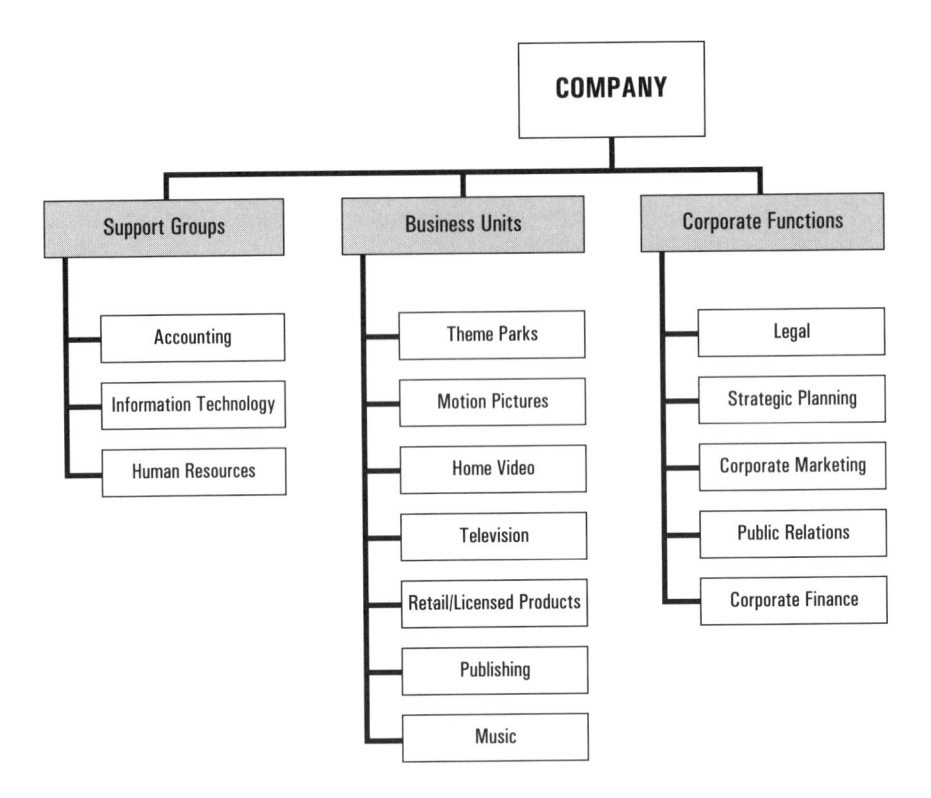

COMPANY

- **Support Groups**
  - Accounting
  - Information Technology
  - Human Resources

- **Business Units**
  - Theme Parks
  - Motion Pictures
  - Home Video
  - Television
  - Retail/Licensed Products
  - Publishing
  - Music

- **Corporate Functions**
  - Legal
  - Strategic Planning
  - Corporate Marketing
  - Public Relations
  - Corporate Finance

Case Study: Independent Filmmaking, Strategic Marketing

Company: IMAX

Project: Create a marketing plan

IMAX is a Canadian educational technology company, primarily known for its visually arresting big screen high-definition films that are exhibited in special theaters, science museums and other educational venues around the world. While fairly lucrative – the company's annual revenues are in the neighborhood of $100 million – it is relatively "small potatoes" within the film industry (a major studio blockbuster can make that much in a few weeks). That said, however, the company has strong brand awareness and promising brand affinity.

While most of the company's revenue is drawn from educational visits, IMAX was seeking to replicate the spectacular success of *Everest* (released in 1998), arguably the most broadly-appealing and highest-grossing of its films, which told the tale of scaling the world's highest peak. While its success was unique in that the movie happened to coincide with the release of the best-selling book *Into Thin Air*, executives believed that with an appropriate marketing and public relations campaign, the movie's success could be duplicated.

To investigate promising revenue opportunities, marketers were asked to do the following: Investigate opportunities to provide schools with learning materials for upcoming releases – both what content would be interesting to students and teachers, and how they would distribute it profitably; create brochures and promotional materials for mailings; orchestrate previews and excitement-generating events; work with publishers to potentially co-brand and launch supplementary books; and measure the breadth of the brand's audience.

Gathering this data required the resources of the company's entire marketing department and several market research firms for over a year. The company has since embarked upon numerous extensions of its franchise and created a solid marketing campaign that it plans to execute in coming seasons.

A Day in the Life of an Inventory Planning Manager

At any company that has a product to distribute, there's somebody who serves as the liaison with the different facets of the company. Here, an insider at a major publishing house provides a look at a typical day as an inventory planning manager.

The basics in publishing are that an editor will sign a book and the author will write it. Many people know this part of the business. However, that's just a portion of what happens.

The publishing company has to determine when the book will be released and how many books will go on the market initially. Also, there is the issue of keeping track of the sales, determining when to reprint or take a book out of print. These operational issues are what I handle.

8:30 a.m.: Arrive – check e-mail and voice mail. One of the e-mails I get gives me the top 100 sales. I check the list and make sure that we have inventory on those titles. If we don't, I'll order a reprint.

10:00 a.m.: I usually have a conference call with the binderies, which is where they bind the books. I make sure that my books are running on schedule and arriving on time. If they're backed up, I prioritize with them which books are the most important for us so that they know which books to produce and in what order.

11:00 a.m.: I have an inventory managers meeting where all the inventory managers discuss issues like any problems, which books are hot or any warehouse issues that come up. The meeting is with the Vice President of Productions and the Vice President of Operations. We sort of clue each other in on both ends, so if there are any problems that come up we can sit down and resolve them together.

Noon: Depending on the day, I'll have a reprint meeting. I'll sit down with the Chief Publisher, associate publishers and marketers. We discuss which titles should be reprinted and in what quantity.

1:00 p.m.: Go to lunch. A lot of times, I'll work through lunch and just keep my door closed so I can get some work done without being bothered. I get my food from the cafeteria.

2:00 p.m.: There are six people who work in conjunction with me, so I'll sit down with the production department and assign due dates and a production order.

3:30 p.m.: I get on the phone with the warehouse and resolve any delivery issues or pricing issues. Any problems that they're having, we'll try to resolve together.

I spend the rest of the afternoon dedicated to any projects I have, such as determining initial print runs or pricing, depending on the day. For example: Before school started, I figured out what back-to-school titles were needed and what quantity. Right now, I'm working on Easter and Valentine's Day titles.

5:30 p.m.: I go home. Occasionally I take work home. Most work is down on an internal network at the office. If I have reports to print or something urgent, I'll take it home, but that only happens once or twice a month.

A Day in the Life of a Strategic Planning Entertainment Executive

While there's no "typical" day, below are some of the most common tasks in Strategic Planning:

- Interfacing with other business units, domestically and abroad, either in calls or in meetings (25%)
- Presentations to the senior executive team on key decisions (25%)
- Presentations from the business units on growth initiatives within other groups (10%)
- Responding to requests from senior management (25%)
- Managing junior team members (15%)

If this sounds murky or unclear, read on for an illustration of the specifics. Overall, the hours are long. There are often stories of many executives who do not have families or children, or often forsake them for their careers.

7:00 a.m.: Arrive at work, make conference calls to Europe to discuss progress on a major new initiative to expand in Europe.

8:00 a.m.: Breakfast meeting with a manager in another business unit, to update one another on work and "keep both ears close to the ground."

9:00 a.m.: Review a subordinate's presentation, assigned last night. The presentation is due early tomorrow for the CEO – revisions must be made with haste.

10:00 a.m.: Return some morning phone calls. Glance at e-mail for anything urgent.

10:30 a.m.: Leave for an off-site meeting to discuss what to do with a waning division in which the top chief just left.

10:45 a.m.: Call my assistant. Have her type up e-mail responses to some new e-mails and send them off on my behalf.

10:55 a.m.: Arrive at off-site meeting. Listen to presentations from key leaders on what to do next.

12:00 p.m.: Depart for lunch meeting with a senior VP at another small entertainment company to propose an acquisition.

1:30 p.m.: Return to office to debrief with CFO on the numbers needed for a 5-year plan.

3:00 p.m.: Answer e-mails, review daily trade publications, *The Hollywood Reporter* and *Daily Variety*.

3:45 p.m.: For fun and to build team morale, respond to office pool on what the weekend's box office will be.

3:47 p.m.: Spontaneous meeting with CEO in the hallway – turns out the presentation originally due tomorrow is not that urgent.

4:00 p.m.: Tell junior manager to call off work and go home since she's been pulling all-nighters for a couple of days.

4:10 p.m.: Start reviewing budget requests and expense reports of department employees.

5:00 p.m.: Peruse the proposals from three top management consulting firms, all vying for a piece of a major project.

6:30 p.m.: Make a conference call to Asia executives to discuss progress on their latest initiative.

7:30 p.m.: Answer all outstanding e-mails.

8:30 p.m.: Leave the office.

Media MBAs

Not long ago, the creative types in media kept a wary eye on the suits or the bean counters, as the business side of media is known. For years, Wall Street paid little attention to the media biz, an industry it didn't take that seriously. Now, with the rise of the global conglomerates and the aftermath of dot-com meltdown, many media professionals, both on the creative and business sides, are finding it necessary to pursue an MBA.

A New Order

"When we started, I had two courses and we had about 40 people in each. Today, in any given semester we have about 400 to 500 students taking one or more classes," says Al Lieberman, Executive Director of NYU Stern's Entertainment, Media and Technology Initiative. Started in 1996, Stern's EMT program awards a certificate to those students who complete at least nine credits in courses like Entertainment Finance and The Business of Sports Marketing. Over at Fordham Business School, Dr. Everette Dennis, Chair of the Communications and Media Management program has also seen an increased interest over the last couple of years, "We have a relatively small program, but we've had probably a 20 to 25 percent increase in applications." Fordham's program, believed to be one of the first in the country, began in the mid-80s when Arthur Taylor, a former president of CBS, arrived as the business school's new dean and brought in William Small, another CBS executive, to head up the program.

So why are more and more media professionals interested in an MBA? Of course, many can argue that a wave of dot-com dropouts have decided to hide out in business school in the wake of the collapse of the dot-coms and the weak ad market. Lieberman argues that this is no trend. "It's a fundamental change because the competitive factors that are driving this are not going away. They are intensifying." He is talking about the shakeup of the media landscape. Deregulation and mergers have given rise to media behemoths.

Technology, without a doubt, has wrought havoc in the industry, forcing firms to rethink their business strategies. That's one reason why Jason Oberlander, a first-year student at Columbia Business School, has found the business side of media so attractive. "The technology that comes out, it's coming out so quickly that it requires people who are able to adapt and think on their feet and are able to pursue new opportunities in order to be successful and compete effectively."

Consumers today have a rainbow of media products to choose from. Dennis says the media industry has become an important economic engine and Wall Street has taken notice. "All of the sudden this was an industry to be reckoned with." Lieberman points to a shift towards cooperation and the building of alliances as well, in an industry that has been notoriously competitive. The current negotiations between CNN and ABC News would have been unheard of just ten years ago. Not only has media seen enormous domestic growth, but abroad as well; says Lieberman, "For every dollar that is generated in the United States, 15 years ago the most they could look for was maybe 25 cents outside, as an export. Now it is dollar for dollar."

What Does An MBA Really Offer?

"A few years ago, I would have said, 'An MBA that would be nice, but it really isn't necessary.' Now, I think an MBA, or at least some exposure to business practices, is probably essential," says Dennis. He cites a growing need for better understanding of market research, audiences, how to manage change and the cash position of a company. In the mid-80s, Lieberman started a marketing firm focused on entertainment and media. At the time, he couldn't find enough qualified candidates to keep pace with the growth of the firm. He ended up recruiting people right out of one of the courses he was teaching at NYU. "I taught this course that I created, called The Marketing of Entertainment Industries at the NYU School of Continuing Education. Out of the 40 or 45 adults that would come in from all kinds of industries to learn about this, I'd pick one or two that were the best and offer them jobs."

Oberland left Showtime as a Communications Manager in Sports and Event Programming, but felt an MBA was the only way to increase his chances for advancement. "I felt that doing the transition within the company would have been difficult. I certainly would have had to take a significant step down in title and in compensation." Dennis concurs that an MBA is increasingly becoming a requirement for management in media companies. "I think people on the creative side are not going to move into major management and executive roles unless they either get this kind of background and experience on their own in some way, or they go to a business school and get it where it is taught systematically."

Bridging the Gap

"One of the biggest problems was the business people who stepped into this world of creativity, didn't understand the creative product, didn't understand how it made money, didn't understand how to apply the basic strategic thinking, therefore there was a huge disconnect," says Lieberman. It takes two to tango, and the creative side has also contributed to the disconnect. Fordham, recognizing the interest by some creative folks to bridge this gap, will be launching a new MS program soon, "It's really tailored to the people from the creative side who do need to know and understand more about business." Stern is also helping the business types better understand the creative process by encouraging Stern students to take courses in filmmaking at the Tisch School of the Arts. "They're not going to make films, but at least they understand the skills, so they don't come on a set and make complete idiots of themselves." At the end of the day, Oberland argues that you need the overall package to get ahead. "I think someone who balances the creative skills with business skills is the most suitable person to run a business from a general management standpoint."

Use the Internet's
MOST TARGETED
job search tools.

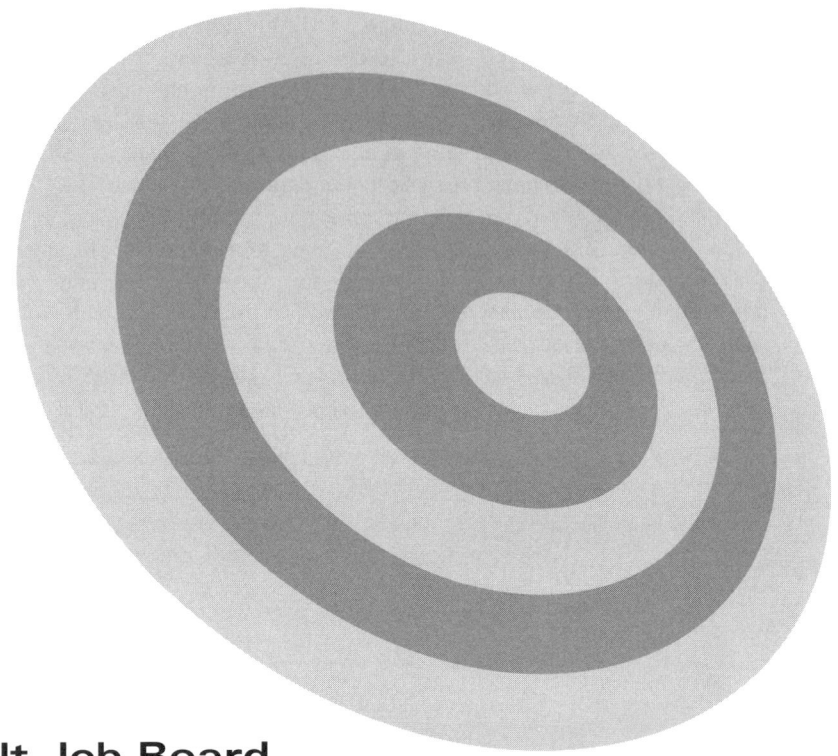

Vault Job Board

Target your search by industry, function, and experience level, and find the job openings that you want.

VaultMatch Resume Database

Vault takes match-making to the next level: post your resume and customize your search by industry, function, experience and more. We'll match job listings with your interests and criteria and e-mail them directly to your inbox.

VAULT
> the insider career network™

The Creative Side: The Jobs

CHAPTER 8

Media companies were previously completely vertically integrated businesses with big conglomerates in control of everything – talent, content and distribution. But because of regulatory changes that broke up this top-to-bottom control, studios, record labels and other major entertainment companies now primarily exist to finance films or to provide the monetary backing for an endeavor. Production companies or independent record labels, with smaller groups of individuals who are relied upon to leverage their personal networks, actually devise the projects that the big companies finance. Actors, directors, singers and entertainers are today all free agents, with union support, more varied opportunities and a larger slice of the pie.

A key difference between the business and creative sides is that established job paths are rare. While there are books written on each of the positions described below, not to mention the copious degree programs dedicated to many of them at universities around the country, here are some quick high-level overviews for beginners. More serious jobseekers should consult the references listed in the back of this guide. While the listings below are not exhaustive of every job that exists, below are many of the most popular ones.

15 Popular Jobs

Studios – development

At every studio, there are those that have the power of the purse strings, the princes and princesses of major projects that have the ability to anoint an endeavor as being "green light" (a go-ahead for financing and execution). They meet with production company executives, writers, directors, make sure that the slate of endeavors for a given year are balanced, address multiple agendas and have an action plan to deliver dollars to the studios. They are responsible for a complete roster – big releases, indies, potential Oscar winners and star vehicles. Assembling this roster is often a delicate balancing act. To get a star to appear in a potential blockbuster, a studio, for instance, may need to guarantee funding for a star's pet project.

Development executives also ensure distribution, work on the scripts of movies they ultimately produce, purchase new scripts and shepherd movies and TV shows through the production cycle. All in all, this is a fun and envy-inducing job if you can land one – it is after all, making movies. The downside is dealing with the lack of job security and the competitive nature of the business.

Producer

Production companies fuel the creative juices in Hollywood. They solicit scripts, pay money for them, gather talent to execute them and essentially bring entertainment to life and life to entertainment. Once a personality has made a name for himself/herself either as an actor, director, writer or producer, he/she will often cut deals (the oft-heard "three-picture deals") where a studio guarantees that it gets first dibs on the person's next project in exchange for providing that person with an office, a staff and discretionary funds to allocate to their very own production company. This is essentially Hollywood's modern-day equivalent of locking in creative talent. In the old days, studios would have exclusive deals with certain actors and actresses, who would then get relatively little (compared to today) for their performances. Old-timers and film buffs refer to the era of studio control over talent as the "star system" era. In contrast, many of today's prominent actors, actresses and directors (Julia Roberts, Tom Hanks, Tom Cruise, Meg Ryan, etc.), as well as countless others who believe they are prominent, have their own production companies.

Many production companies are located on the lots of the major film studios and have small staffs of about a dozen people supporting them, mainly a combination of development executives and assistants. They meet daily with writers and directors, read countless movie scripts from aspiring and established writers (called "spec scripts"), read books by new authors, distribute suggestions ("notes") on improving scripts to writers and look for projects to get off the ground. Often the types of projects that get off the ground are those that are the pet projects of the head of the production company (perhaps someone wants to do a military drama or a teen comedy) but occasionally some are creative projects that are able to rise above the clutter purely on their own merits. Independent production companies (those not affiliated with a studio) are often very good at looking for content that stands on its own.

Once a potential project is spotted, it is a development executive's job to then solicit a complete package – a camera-ready script that has been polished by a prominent script doctor (usually an already established Hollywood screenwriter), a director, and other actors. Rewrites, by the way, form the bulk of income for A-list writers.) Only when a movie has star power "attached" to it will it stand a chance of being funded by the studio. The personal networks of those at production companies are therefore perhaps the biggest assets that studios pay for, because they are the ones that can assure that a film gets made.

While on its face, it is a glamorous job, it is also tough because it is hard to penetrate, jobs are scarce, success rates are low and there is plenty of pressure because hits are harder to generate than it seems. "I don't know that I'll ever make a hit," lamented one D-girl, the notorious nickname for the numerous youngish females in the development world. The upside is that once a movie actually gets a green light, there's usually no turning back, especially once filming has commenced. And if a film ultimately is released, there is the glory that comes with one of the numerous producer credits that come at the beginning of the movie and poise a person for his/her next project. Of course, the really, really big upside if you are extraordinarily lucky is to stand on stage and accept a Best Picture Oscar. The challenge is that most films, even after overcoming the hurdles of being produced, are not even good enough to perform well at the box office.

Compared to movie studios, jobs are a bit easier to come by at any of the numerous production companies than at movie studios, but they are by no means easy to get.

Studios – marketing

Once filming on a movie has wrapped, the post-production machine starts. This includes all the editing, special effects, music, sound and finishing touches that complete the picture. During this time, the marketing machine for movies also starts. There are several different components of film marketing. The first is the creative – the ads and posters that publicize a movie. Film ads are usually called trailers, with excerpts from the movies and often with testimonials from viewers or reviewers. Posters are called one-sheets and are quick eye-catching visual images with one-liners that tease audiences and tell them the big names involved in a film.

On the creative side, trailers and one-sheets (posters) are rarely executed by individuals within the studio. Trailers are handed over to freelancers at independent post-production companies called trailer houses, though on occasion they are controlled by the director or producer of the movie. One-sheets are typically the product of freelancers from ad agencies who have been closely directed by a movie director, a studio executive and sometimes a movie marketer.

Film marketing typically involves two key tasks: determining a media budget and the allocation of placement in TV, print, and radio through media agencies like Western, and conducting research and tracking studies to understand who sees different movies, how they test before sample audiences and how people respond to different movies. More recently, movie marketers have taken on the role of salesmen, similar to the licensing division of consumer products, where they seek complimentary partners to promote a film and defray costs of promotion (e.g. BMW with MGM's James Bond franchise, McDonald's with any Disney animated release). Movie marketers also create web sites that support the launch of a film.

Movie marketing is an interesting career path for anyone interested in combining classical marketing training with the entertainment industry. Additionally, there are the requisite perks that accompany the job – early viewings of upcoming movies, occasional tickets to film premieres, etc.

Entertainment publicist

Entertainment publicists are PR agents for entertainment companies. They manage music, TV and movie stars, coordinating their public appearances including award shows, parties and TV appearances and interviews, often accompanying them on the red carpet or on press tours. Entertainment PR firms are mostly small firms owned by individual PR agents with enormous personal networks. The most famous ones are Wolf-Kasteller, Rogers & Cowan and Baker-Winokur-Ryder. In general, these firms extract far more fees from business clients than from celebrities – typically, celebrity fees are a fraction of corporate fees.– but the celebrities give them exposure and publicity for themselves.

Talent agent

Agents are like accountants. No one particularly likes them, but you've got to have one. They're the only ones that know all the intricacies of the TV/music/film industry, can help you navigate the process of finding a job, and are the ones in the best position to get you what you want.

Most actors, musicians and writers have agents. An agent is usually a very connected person who negotiates deals. Agents typically charge a fixed commission of around 10 percent. They get writers accepted onto TV shows, they get actors cast, and, often, they serve as therapeutic sounding boards and friends.

There are primarily two types of agents – talent agents, who represent actors, musicians and directors, and literary agents, who represent the writers and authors that create the blueprints for the stories that get developed into films. There are countless agencies throughout Hollywood, but there are only a handful that handle A-list actors, directors and writers. The main ones are Creative Artists Agency (CAA), International Creative Management (ICM), William Morris and United Talent Agency (UTA). CAA was the first big mega-agency, started by Hollywood legend and failed corporate executive Michael Ovitz. Endeavor is one of the newest ones, started as an exodus of ex-ICM agents who formed their own group of young power-hitters.

Agents are also famous for handling interference for stars and prominent personalities. For example, if a studio, or a production company wants a star, the agent takes the call and relays info to that star – the notorious "let my people talk to your people." If a famous person wants something, usually they have their personal assistant (or occasionally their agent) call. If someone is not famous, a good agent can make phone calls to get someone at a studio or production company to take their call. Agents are the people who bring together different people in the industry – the wheeler-dealers for those who aren't as skilled at networking for themselves. While agencies draw many prospective employees, it takes a certain kind of person with a certain thick skin to stay. It's essentially a sales job. There are tons of agents around and it is highly competitive. The industry abounds with endless stories of individuals who finish law school and start in the mail rooms at talent agencies.

However, agencies are one of the best places to start because of the volume of people one meets and the contacts one gains by working there. It's hard work, even abusive at times, but it is the best way to break into the entertainment world, especially for those with few other connections.

Director

The director of a motion picture, television show or theatrical production is the conductor, the driver, the maestro of the performance. Directors orchestrate musical performances for television videos, television shows for network TV, ads for commercials and, of course, films for release in theaters. A successful director takes on the roles of visionary, acting coach, dorm parent and savvy businessperson. While the rewards are often enticing (everyone in Hollywood ultimately wants to direct), it is also a rare individual who can pull it all off properly. Even among directors, few break out as the geniuses of their generation – most churn out undistinguished productions.

The path to becoming a director almost always involves some film school training. There are hundreds of programs throughout the country that will enable you to shoot some footage and provide an editing facility to put something together, but there are few with the clout to land you major jobs. Even USC, UCLA and NYU film school graduates report struggling to find their first paying gigs, even with acclaimed shorts and pieces.

Web designer

Web designers are important because Internet marketing is an increasingly important component of a film, TV show or album's marketing budget and strategy. At the same time, it is a young field where there are opportunities for creativity and the integration of one's artistic talents.

Web designers are often hired on a freelance basis as part of advertising agencies or graphics houses, but more and more of them are being integrated into the fold of studio payrolls due to cost concerns. The constant media blitzes of new properties force daily upkeeps of entertainment web sites due to marketing contests, lead generation tools, e-mails, streaming media and Web-based marketing. Additionally, as movies become more sophisticated and laden with special effects and computer-generated imagery, the Web becomes a tool for promoting and showcasing these features beyond the marketing during a film trailer or TV commercial.

Post production

Post production is everything that happens to a film once shooting ends and the cast and crew go home. It involves the editors who work with sophisticated computer technology to put together hundreds of hours of raw footage into a cohesive and exciting story; it is the musicians who compose the score, it the sound effects editors and Foley artists who add image-enhancing sounds when the original noise was not sufficient and it is countless other assistants and project managers who make up the latter half of a film's credits.

These technical positions are often unionized and require several years of apprenticeship before accreditation. Upon being formally inducted into a union, a person is eligible for union wages. Procuring jobs is often based on who one knows – directors often select teams for their films who they worked with in the past. Those relationships end up being extremely valuable since people often work with the same individuals again and again. Many post-production artists are film school graduates that either specialized in coursework related to one particular area, or are people who were brought into apprenticeship programs through friends.

Crew

The "crew" of any production is the behind-the-scenes individuals who work on the set of a movie, film, TV show, or video production. This is separate from the "cast," the actors or performers in front of the camera. There are often intriguing titles in a film's credits (e.g. boom operator, best boy, grips, etc.). They also include the usual expected characters – the costume designers, the makeup artists, the hairdressers and so on.

The most important members of a crew (aside from the director of course) is the cinematographer, a.k.a. the director of photography (more commonly known as the DP). This is the individual that creates the visual texture of the film and makes each scene aesthetically appealing. Boom operators, grips, and best boys are often the "muscles" behind a production – generally men who work with the technical details of sound, projection, lighting and other aspects of production.

There are a few other key roles – one is the Assistant Director and the Unit Production Manager. The AD works with the director, and often has the opportunity to direct secondary footage (establishing shots, the introductory credits and transition scenes). The Unit Production Manager manages the logistics of making everything happen for the director – ensuring that the location is suited for shooting, that all permits have been met, that everyone working on the set is doing so within union guidelines, managing payroll and the shooting schedule, ensuring that catering and ancillary benefits for the cast and crew are accommodated and making sure that all the requisite production necessities are on hand (i.e., trailers for stars, headphones and walkie-talkies, etc.).

The lowest level of entry onto the set of a production is as a production assistant. Any given production will have about a half-dozen PAs, some paid, others not. Many of them will be friends of crew members who simply want credits on their entertainment resumes. PAs are the production parallel of creative assistants. They deliver scripts to relevant parties, fetch coffee and do any other menial tasks that need to be done.

As in post-production positions, most crew members are unionized. For those fortunate enough to be in the loop, it can be a glamorous job that enables a person to travel to exotic locations for film shoots, enjoy several months of vacation a year in between projects and earn a healthy salary in the process. The downside, of course, is that projects are uncertain and the hours are very long while working (film shoots are known for being pressured sessions of 14 hour days for 30 days straight). There are some unique programs to enter the field, such as the Assistant Director Training Program which is sponsored by the Director's Guild of America. About two dozen individuals with some experience in the entertainment industry and with goals of eventually being Unit Production Managers (the title of the program is a bit of a misnomer – the application clearly states that it is not for aspiring directors), are given the opportunity to work for a year on major productions.

A Day in the Life of a Creative Executive

As on the business side, there is no typical day for a creative executive, but there are some key things that every creative exec is entrusted with doing:

- Meet with writers, give feedback (30%)
- Have meetings with other internal executives (10%)
- Meet with producers and studio executives (20%)
- Read scripts and make offers to option books (20%)
- Talk to agents (20%)

Here is an example of a typical day:

7:30 a.m.: Power breakfast with fellow development executive with whom you once answered phones.

8:30 a.m.: Check voice mail. Ask assistant to read e-mails to you over the phone on the way in to work.

8:45 a.m.: Call New York literary agent you've been trying to contact for a few days for the rights to a recently released novel.

9:15 a.m.: Ask star's agent to send over a term sheet. Ask assistant to hire a script reader who has called 10 times asking for work. You need to dig into the pile that's next to your desk.

9:15-10:00 a.m.: Look over the term sheet from the agent and call back to negotiate a lower rate. Agent refuses to budge. You say you'll think about it.

10:00 a.m.- 12:00 p.m.: Meeting with a writing duo to give comments on a script that you've just optioned for $20,000. If you can get it polished and get a writer or director attached, you can sell it to a studio.

12:00 p.m.: Leave for lunch across town.

12:15 p.m.: Return calls. Check into tailor for your dress that needs alteration before your black-tie cocktail party next weekend.

12:30 p.m.: Power lunch with studio executive who may be interested in the script you have just optioned.

1:30 p.m.: Ask assistant for Internet research on some names that came up during lunch, potential "script doctors." You make calls to inquire about them further.

2:00 p.m.: Drop by your former literary agency, schmooze with an old friend, now an agent. Get a coffee, talk scripts.

3:00-3:15 p.m.: Back to the office. Listen to voice mail. Respond to e-mails.

3:15-5 p.m.: Try to reach other talent agents about the script. Respond to literary agents who have sent scripts over.

5:00 p.m.: Miss a big call from a producer you're waiting for. Before you explode at your assistant, you find out that the phone didn't even ring – the call went (purposefully) straight to voice mail, presumably to avoid a conversation but to communicate the guise of trying to call. You call back, only to get more voice mail. Make a note to try again tomorrow.

5:20-7:00 p.m.: Read new scripts sent over – the ones not handed over to the script reader. Look over coverage to see if anything interesting pops. One has potential for something that Brad Pitt's agent said he was looking for, but it's too poorly written to investigate further.

7 p.m.: Leave for dinner and drinks with another producer.

Creative assistant

While widely regarded as the bottom, the legendary dregs of the pool, this is the starting point for any career launch into the creative side of the industry. Cynics say assistants are there to feed the egos of self-important creative executives, but others assert that it is a rite of passage to the brotherhood (and sisterhood) of entertainment, not to mention a good training ground for the next generation of creative executives.

The typical job of a creative assistant is to do everything from fetching coffee to kids from one's boss' day care, answering hundreds of calls on a daily basis and making dinner reservations for one's manager, to occasionally, if there is time, reading scripts and writing coverage. (See Survival Tips for Assistants for more.)

Screenwriter

The screenplay is the blueprint for a movie. With virtually no barriers to entry in creating a script, there are many people who aspire to create screenplays. You can take classes, buy books, even get software that promises to help you write the screenplay. Furthermore, Hollywood makes the same formulas over and over again – how hard could it possible be?

However, be forewarned that of the thousands that try, there are only a few that are able to make a living writing.

The market is quirky, and unknown writers have difficulty getting their manuscripts read. Word of mouth and buzz help tremendously. If someone hears that one script may be getting action, that often starts a bidding war, even if a person may have read and passed on the same script before.

Script reader

Given the sheer volume of aspiring writers churning out scripts every year, it is often a cumbersome task for a single creative executive to analyze them all. Script reading is generally a stepping stone.

Professional script readers work with production companies to review the loads of prospective scripts that enter through the company's doors every day. A reader then gets approximately $50 to write a synopsis and to give an opinion on whether or not it should move forward.

Script readers for studios are even more institutionalized, as is everything in Hollywood. Such individuals for studios are actually unionized, and those jobs are much more difficult to procure due to those restrictions.

Trade publishing editor

These are the professionals who actually decide what books a publishing house will print. They take solicitations from agents, sign authors, then work to prepare the book for publication. They also work with artists and marketers to assure that there is appropriate publicity and that the book jacket is appealing.

TV programming

TV programming professionals monitor Nielsen ratings, decide what stays on the air and tweak scripts.. These are the people that determine what a network's schedule looks like. Often, they come from market research backgrounds because market research is much of what TV programming is – monitoring what people say about programs and responding accordingly. These positions are diminishing, as there is really only room for TV programming professionals at major networks.

The smaller channels rely on program directors and raw Nielsen scores to make decisions. They also are more likely to tinker with the actual shows than with scheduling. Smaller channels experiment more with shows, because they have limited budgets and it is much cheaper to produce shows than pilots. Smaller channels only produce a few shows in-house, and are committed to getting these shows made, shot and shown. To fill up the rest of their airtime, they purchase rights to air other already established shows.

A Day in the Life of a Network News Producer

9:00 a.m.: Get into the office. Check e-mail and voice mail. If there are any issues that need immediate attention, deal with them right away.

9:30 a.m.: Read a variety of national papers, including *The New York Times*, *Los Angeles Times*, *Washington Post* and *The Boston Globe* to look for story ideas. Scan the latest wires to see what stories are shaping up for the day.

10:00 a.m.: Review the status of assigned stories. Determine what needs to get done that day and what can wait.

10:10 a.m.: Send an e-mail to associate producer to collect articles on an interview subject for tomorrow.

11:00 a.m.: Publicity meeting with Executive Producer, publicist, affiliate relations and web producer to discuss how to promote a piece that's airing in this week's show.

11:45 a.m.: Set up camera crew for tomorrow's shoot. Make sure cameraman has details, so she knows what equipment she will need.

12:15 p.m.: Call back legal department to see if the rights to a piece of music that will appear in this week's story have been cleared for use.

12:30 p.m.: Grab lunch.

1:00 p.m.: Review the research from the associate producer and develop questions for tomorrow's interview with a doctor. E-mail suggested questions to correspondent.

1:45 p.m.: Call back a publicist who is pitching an author as a story idea.

2:15 p.m.: Sit with the editor who is cutting a piece that will air in four days.

5 p.m.: Leave for camera shoot downtown at a blues club for a profile of a singer airing in two weeks.

5:30 p.m.: Manager of club starts giving cameraman a hard time about where to set up. Work with publicist and manager of club to find best solution as to the position of the camera, so the audiences' view is unobstructed.

5:45 p.m.: Find the sound person in the club, so cameraman can plug into the soundboard for best sound.

6:30 p.m.: Review with cameraman the shots that are needed for story.

7 p.m.: Show starts.

8:30 p.m.: Show ends. It's a wrap for the day.

A&R Rep

Artist & repertoire (A&R) representatives are essentially the talent scouts that travel the country to discover the 'N Syncs, the Ricky Martins and the Britney Spears. They listen to demo tapes, they audition singers for new bands (if they're trying to create them), they go to concerts, they listen for new sounds and try to find appropriate people to illustrate them. They're the talent agents scouting out the fresh new faces that can be made into stars. Some are independent, but many are often employed by music studios. Even when they find people, there are several layers of executives who must approve the talent before cutting a record deal. The music industry is similar to Hollywood in that there are rosters, and established acts are a big part of sales, but there are also some newer acts that can be categorized into different groups. For the most part, the record industry is highly fragmented, with the Big Five labels making the most money, but with many much smaller labels that target niche audiences.

Day in the Life of a Senior News Editor at a Major News Magazine

I work out of a domestic bureau office, so I don't have a boss or a supervisor. In terms of an editorial staff, there is myself and maybe five other writers, a business writer, and a photo editor. My schedule really varies week to week and month to month. It's always kind of like learning something new.

I usually get in around 10 a.m.

I read the papers, check e-mails, drink my coffee. I put a lot of pressure on myself to know what's going on in all aspects of the world because I don't have a specific beat. I read really fast. I read the online sites of some of the major publications to get a broad overview of what's going on. I'm basically a content addict – I read anything and everything.

Mid-morning

I have four or five sources to call. I do a lot of phone interviews. A lot of it is person to person contact – tracking people down. Learning enough about them to interview them. I'll interview anyone from CEOs of corporations to criminals.

I also have about five or six articles I'm working on. I spend a lot of time reading clips and primary source material, then taking notes on it for my articles. I'm fortunate that I don't have a specific beat; I don't want to tie myself down to any specific thing at this point.

Story-time afternoons

In terms of writing, it varies. Sometimes it's spot news, which I do in a very short time. The smallest story I do is a one column – those are things you can pound out in a day. A cover story might take anywhere from four weeks to three months. I do dozens and dozens of interviews (for a cover story) for about 4,000 words. It's really gathering a bunch of information.

A one-to-two page story is typical. I like to spend a week on them. When you put more effort into it, it really shows up on the page.

More notes from our editor insider

Deadlines

I'm definitely a procrastinator. I work better under pressure. I become obsessed with the topic.

I have to handle many kinds of stories at once. If I have a long-term cover project, I try to dedicate an hour a day to it. My favorite way of working is having one story. In terms of deadline pressure, I was much more concerned when I first started out here. I spent all this time worrying about it. Deadlines aren't really a problem for me. I put pressure on myself more than anything else.

Travel writing

I love to travel. I'm usually traveling (on business) about a quarter of the time. I travel on weekends a lot. I was gone last month for a lot of the month. When you travel you live your story and hang out with your sources. Once, I was out on a treasure hunt in North Carolina; that was a job that was fun! You can only be one person, but by being a journalist or writer you can really get a taste of other people's lives. How they deal with situations that I face. I'm addicted to stories. You realize that there's stories going on all the time. Being a writer is a way to attack those and be involved.

Wrapping it up

I work typically 10 hours a day. There are times when I spend less, and times when I spend more. There have been times I've been here until one (in the morning). The job is never done. I have a little home office, and I'm sure I'll go home tonight and do some reading. There's a personal element to my reading, but that's where my story ideas come from. When I'm at home reading, that's when the lights go on in my head. I do a lot of writing in the evening, when it's quiet.

How a Movie Gets Made

Step		Players/Functions	Phase
1	Movie "blueprint" created	Players: Screenwriter	Development Hell
2	Agent (or writer) brings script to a producer or studio executive	Players: Screenwriter; Screenwriter's Agent/Lawyer/Manager; Producer; Studio Executive	Development Hell
3	Producer "attaches" stars and takes it to a studio	Players: Producer; Studio Executive; Actors/Director; (Stars); Agents for Stars	Development Hell
4	Movie "green lit"; complete cast/crew recruited	Players: Producer; Secondary Cast and Crew; Agents/Lawyers/Managers for Secondary Cast and Crew	Pre-Production
5	Budget set, timeline created, filming begins	Players: Producer; Director; Stars; Secondary Cast and Crew	Production
6	Finishing touches added	Functions: Editing, Sound Effects, Credits	Post-Production
7	Publicity starts after "rough cut" is complete	Functions: Audience Testing, PR Junket, Press Tour, Movie Trailers Launched, Other Marketing	Post-Production

Film is released in theaters

VAULT CAREER GUIDES
GET THE INSIDE SCOOP ON TOP JOBS

"Cliffs Notes for Careers"
– *FORBES MAGAZINE*

Vault guides and employer profiles have been published since 1997 and are the premier source of insider information on careers.

Each year, Vault surveys and interviews thousands of employees to give readers the inside scoop on industries and specific employers to help them get the jobs they want.

"To get the unvarnished scoop, check out Vault"
– *SMARTMONEY MAGAZINE*

VAULT

Survival Skills for Assistants

CHAPTER 9

Being an assistant is the first rung up the entertainment ladder. Here are some tips for getting and keeping these jobs – and setting yourself up to move up beyond the assistant level.

Getting in

While assistants are the proverbial low men on the creative totem pole, they are nonetheless difficult positions to land because there are a fixed number of spots and openings are rare. A position becomes available only when people are promoted, fired or quit. Furthermore, it is the starting place for everyone, so the competition is quite tough. Even experienced business executives with MBAs who want to transition to the creative side are unable to avoid becoming a CA. Throughout the media and entertainment world are countless former attorneys, accountants and other aspiring professionals.

The most popular way of breaking into an assistant position is through referrals. Others break in through cold calls. Still others penetrate the ranks by making friends with other assistants and then patiently trolling for the next job opening. Some CAs migrate from a low-status boss to a higher-status boss, remaining in the assistant ranks for many years.

The interview

The interview for an assistant position is usually intended to assess one's humility, modesty and overall industriousness. There will be the inevitable questions that inquire into one's general tolerance in gruntwork. Often, it takes the form of the following question: "But you're overqualified for this job – won't you get bored?" Beware. The point of the question is to question your dedication to tiring, detailed work. A good answer will showcase your intelligence while pointing out that you are not only capable, but eager, willing and very able to execute even the most menial of tasks with alacrity and aplomb. Typical tasks that are the domain of assistants are answering phones, running errands and accepting a less-than-ideal lifestyle. You need to persuade your interviewer, who is unlikely to be the person you will work for (Hollywood types often prefer to forego meeting with the "little people"), that you will do anything and everything that's asked and required of you, and then some. You will be told about your benefits (few to none) and your pay. Do not flinch or waver in any way. It will be construed as a sign of weakness!

Occasionally, an interviewer will ask you for your "coverage," which is essentially a synopsis and analysis of a script. Assistants are sometimes entrusted with the responsibility of writing coverage on scripts, and any previous experience writing such coverage can prove to one's advantage. If you don't have any coverage experience, an interviewer will sometimes give you a script and ask that you provide your written comments on it.

Managing your boss

The position of assistant encompasses such duties as secretary, butler, chauffer, mother and confidante. For all the books ever written on management skills, they are all but irrelevant in the entertainment industry. Rarely will you aggregate a larger group of individuals who care less about developing others. One executive described the junior ranks as "suckling on the teats of wolves."

The most important traits of successful assistants are:

Flexibility. Many assistants are required to juggle and reprioritize their own lives in order to accommodate their managers. One assistant tells of missing a flight out for a vacation because the manager called inquiring about some small bit of information that the assistant was supposed to have had.

Patience. Many assistants report countless evenings of waiting around in the office long after the boss had left to a leisure dinner with "business partners." Many managers often tell their underlings to wait until they they are told to go home. Usually the request is legitimized by the (flimsy) guise of receiving a phone call that must be immediately patched through.

Resourcefulness. Often, it is the assistant's responsibility to unearth obscure tidbits of information or to seek out some difficult-to-find object. Whether it reservations at 8 p.m. on a Friday night for the most popular restaurant in town or a rare edition, out-of-print book, assistants are often expected to find ways to make difficult things happen.

Indulgence. The assistant is also expected to be kind and proactive – remembering birthdays and special occasions, congratulating successes and commiserating failures. The best assistants are known for anticipating special requests, accommodating the quirks of their managers, before the manager asks. "I'll try to get my boss his favorite latte every morning if he's unable to pick one up for himself," says one assistant at a prominent Hollywood talent agency.

Eagerness. Cheerfulness and a positive attitude, even in the face of adversity, is vital in the profession. The grumpy are quickly replaced with those more eager and willing.

Making the most of low wages

Assistants make anywhere from $20,000 per year to above $45,000. Usually, the higher paid assistants are in the coveted positions of working at a studio in a unionized position. The majority of assistants earn a salary near the lower end of the spectrum. In order to sustain a viable lifestyle, most assistants resort to the usual manners of making ends meet – sharing living expenses with roommates in modest neighborhoods, limiting indulgences on food (ordering in on the company's dime whenever possible), cutting back expenses on clothing and entertainment, investing in modest transport, borrowing funds from parents. Despite the low salaries, there are often perks to the profession that should not be overlooked. Many assistants manage to allay some of their expenses on staples like dry cleaning by leveraging the generous expense accounts of their managers. Others engage in supplementary income sources, such as teaching on weekends, in order to increase their cash flow.

Getting promoted

If you stick it out long enough in a CA job, you'll probably move up The hard part is waiting it out, often over the course of several years, sacrificing late nights, while making the right connections and waiting for a lucky break. While there are things that can be done – meeting lots of people, keeping your ears and eyes open to opportunities, jumping to a lesser-known company in order to make a transition out of the assistant ranks – promotion ultimately boils down to timing, persistence and good fortune. Good assistants quickly learn to build networks with other assistants, to share information on what's hot in order to give their bosses the extra edge, to religiously listen in on phone calls and to constantly look out for their own best interests.

Becoming a Magazine Editorial Assistant

by Sally Melanie Lourenco

Every magazine has a different number of people on staff. Some features-focused magazines (like *Vanity Fair* and *Conde Nast Traveler*) have mostly copy, features and research editors; fashion publications have large fashion, photo and art departments; and so on. What follows is a general list of entry level editorial, fashion, and art department positions, plus the scoop on getting promoted to the next level.

An introduction to the editorial assistantship

An unspoken rule here is that the level at which you assist has a great bearing on how far you will go and how quickly you will get there. Assisting lower level associate editors, some of whom have just been promoted and given their first-ever assistant, may include more menial tasks and doesn't allow for the direct experience you'd get assisting someone at the executive level.

With most assistant level positions, salaries are usually in the same low range. Executive assistants (usually for an editor-in-chief, who has both editorial and executive assistants), however, get paid almost as much as the assistant editors, in some cases more. But you aren't in it for the money, remember?

Generally, you could be an assistant for anywhere from one to five years before you are promoted from within. It all depends on how much you learn, how fast you master your menial tasks and what kind of changes may be happening within the magazine. If you are given extra editorial writing and editing responsibilities, or if you work for an Executive Editor or Director for 1-2 years, you may be able to score an Assistant Editor's post by moving to another magazine.

The department you choose to work in will have direct bearing on how you move within the magazine. Switching directions just wastes time, so choose wisely. Select something you have a personal interest in and can dedicate yourself to for the long-term.

Responsibilities

You will do grunt work and love it. Filing, opening and sorting mail, faxing, scheduling, expense reports, typing, research, making appointments, copying and anything else that will make the editors' lives easier. You'll need excellent organizational and phone skills, and be responsible for maintaining updated contact lists, juggling the phone, faxing and figuring out which tasks are most important and which you can hold off on in an emergency. When you get promoted to a higher position, your success will depend on just how organized you are and how successful you've been in these areas.

This phase seems never-ending at times, but it prepares you for the mania to come. You definitely need to know Excel, Word and all Microsoft Office suite programs thoroughly. It's a plus if you are familiar with Desktop Publishing software like Quark. You'll also need to know how to draft letters, make charts, and so forth. Even though you may think that personal requests such as dry cleaning, shopping and dinner reservations are not part of your job responsibility, you'll need to realize that attitude is everything. How badly do you want to make your boss' life easier, and how much will you appreciate it when someone does it for you later on?

Salaries start at $23,000 per year plus benefits, and most large magazines pay overtime. There will be a great deal of overtime, so most months it will feel like you're making $30,000 or more.

By job

Editorial assistant

Support one or more editors with daily administrative work. After all that is done, depending on what level editor you work for, you may also: keep contacts with freelance editors; preview and open manuscripts and story proposals; answer reader mail, contribute small 100- to 200-word articles to the magazine; research for feature stories; write headlines and decks; and keep track of story ideas and editorial planning.

Getting Hired

Experience at a school newspaper, magazine or freelance contributions to other smaller local publications are a plus. A journalism and/or English education is also attractive. Also consider the topics covered at the magazine of your choice – news, economics, psychology, fashion etc. Any education or background that could help you come up with relevant topics and ideas is essential. This may even help you specialize in a section such as interior design or business news.

Getting Promoted

If you handle your administrative duties well and balance any writing or editing assignments, you could be promoted to Assistant Editor level in a year. It also depends on whom you work for. If it is an executive-level editor who allows you to take on larger responsibilities, the experience will be invaluable and essential to your promotion within or at another magazine.

Fashion assistant

Responsibilities

Fashion editors and writers conceive and compose stories. For an assistant, duties include administrative work as mentioned, but may include some editing, proofreading, research, caption and headline writing. You may also be able to write small stories and reporting for the Front of Book (all the pages that come before the main feature stories and photo shoots in the middle to back of book. The Front of Book (FOB) usually contains short report-style stories).

Getting Hired

The requirements here are much the same as an editorial assistant. A genuine interest in the magazine you are working for and knowledge of the reader is essential as well. Some editors may ask you to make a list of ideas you'd have for certain FOB sections, just to see how you think. But the main concern is whether or not you will be patient enough to put in the time, do the administrative work and learn slowly. There may also be times when you are called upon to write a larger story, so any clips you have from school publications, or writing samples from essays and reports you've written, would be helpful. An internship is also a plus, as is knowledge of fashion history.

Getting Promoted

Some assistants wait two years, just to be passed over for a position for someone from the outside. Be sure to ask what your prospective employer's policy is on promoting from within. Others are gradually given more reports to write and pages to edit. It all depends on how quickly you work and how well you handle each responsibility, as well as how willing you are to learn the craft. The concern here is not to move up in title, but to accumulate clips and bylines. If you are an assistant who is allowed to write in every issue and consistently given larger assignments, it is beneficial for you to remain where you are until the right opportunity arrives.

Fashion market editors' assistant

There are also fashion market editors' assistants. Here you'll be doing all of the administrative work, including: calling in all the clothes for your editor's markets and assigned shoots (sometimes that means five or six shoots at once), returning all the clothes, keeping track of the items needed and similar tasks. There is a tremendous amount of follow-through involved, so you have to be meticulous. Most of your time will be spent sitting at your desk and returning clothes or accessories from the fashion closet, which means long hours. You will not be going on any appointments unless you have built a solid relationship with your editor and she is willing to let you cover some smaller markets (like sunglasses or lingerie). This usually happens after one year. There will be long hours and tremendous amounts of scheduling. If you love clothes and want to be a market editor, then this is the job for you.

Getting Hired

Market editors look for people who are interested in becoming market editors. Previous work as an executive assistant in fashion will get you in, as will an internship at a major magazine working in the fashion market department. Be professional and polished in attitude and appearance. Market editors are representatives for their magazines and always look the part. A fashion education is not essential. Organization, computer skills and ability to juggle tasks are a plus.

Getting Promoted

I have seen countless assistants become frustrated with the grunt work and long hours associated with this position. Many have left and have been promoted at other types of magazines earlier than they would have been had they stayed in fashion. At fashion magazines, it is all about your boss' attitude and trust. You may start off with small markets like swimwear and lingerie or sunglasses – how well you handle these responsibilities will determine how long it will take to climb. It is a very competitive field. It's always wise to ask up front what the chances are for increased responsibilities.

Stylist's assistant

If you work for a fashion editor who styles shoots, you will be making travel arrangements, packing trunks of clothes, hauling them everywhere you go and keeping track of every last item you take with you. You will also be responsible for returning the items, calling the designers to get items in (although sometimes this is up to the market editors) and keeping track of ideas and ideas boards. You'll also be going on every shoot with the editor. Warning: This is very exciting and attractive to many young aspiring editors because of the glamorous veneer, but it wears off very quickly. Unless you have a genuine interest in photography, models and the visual aspect of the craft, this is not a wise choice. You will be working every day of the week (weekends too), traveling at a moment's notice, waking up at 5 a.m. and going to bed after midnight at times. You have to love it, and realize that you are an assistant – and that most assistants suffer through similar grueling schedules and menial tasks. If you have a large ego and aren't willing to do anything and everything your editor tells you, then you should reconsider pursuing this position.

Getting Hired

Stylists look for proficient, humble, hard-working assistants. You'll be keeping longer hours then they do, and they work long hours, so you need to be dedicated. You will also be working with difficult, cranky photographers and models with major egos at times. To succeed, you must have a calm, patient and diplomatic manner, no matter what is going on around you. It is also common for stylists to request assistants that can commit to the job for more than a year, usually two to three years. Your background should include some work with photographers (perhaps assisting) or with another stylist. Fashion design and photography education are most desirable.

Getting Promoted

After two to three years working with a top-notch stylist at a major fashion publication or a cutting edge magazine, you can go to a smaller publication and style your own shoots. Most assistants begin to freelance on the side for lesser-known publications in order to build a portfolio. Without a portfolio it will take you longer. Be advised that this is tricky – most major companies do not allow employees to freelance (there may be an intellectual property clause in your contract). You could also look for an opportunity to style smaller shoots for your employer – perhaps still life styling. If you have the right eye for your magazine, you may be promoted.

Photo assistant

Administrative responsibilities abound here as well. You'll log in and return film and portfolios, correspond with photographers, assist with travel arrangements for shoots, order prints, prepare expense reports, invoices and budgets, send issues to contributing photographers and organize countless files for the department.

Getting Hired

An interest in photography, especially the type used in the magazine you've chosen, is a must. Knowledge of and an educational background in photography are also beneficial. Being good with numbers and budgets is essential, as are follow-through skills. You may also have to be diplomatic when faced with irate requests from photographers and other editors.

Getting Promoted

After one year you should be able to move up to assistant or associate level, where you'll have direct relationships with photographers, organize shoots, and have developed a good eye for the kind of look your magazine prefers. This takes time, however, and it all depends on how quickly you learn your craft.

Art assistant

You'll probably be doing more administrative follow-up and page proof trafficking here than anything else. There will also be photo research and art research, where you will find pictures and photographs from agencies for relevant pages. Computer proficiency is essential, since you will be using scanners, Quark and Photoshop.

Getting Hired

A BFA and folio of past layouts or design projects you've worked on in school is needed, in addition to extensive knowledge of desktop publishing programs.

Getting Promoted

To get promoted, you will have to master the look of the magazine you work for, and work under someone who allows you added responsibilities with pages. This usually comes after two years. It is an enormous responsibility to manage the total look of a magazine and many places require you to have added education in mastering copy fitting as well as visuals.

Production assistant

You'll be responsible for maintaining the deadline schedules of the magazine and following up on all internal delays, in addition to the typical administrative duties. This department focuses on all stages of editorial production, from beginning concepts, page counts and budgets to final approvals by editors and editors-in-chief. Your job will be to learn this and master it, taking some of the pressure off your supervisor.

Getting Hired

A genuine interest in management and production is essential. Don't take this job as a back door to another department. You have to be extremely organized, willing to work long hours, and able to work well under pressure and when things go wrong. Knowledge of Quark and Photoshop is also a plus.

Getting Promoted

After a solid year at this job, you may be able to demonstrate the responsibility and attention to warrant a promotion. It really depends on how much your supervisor thinks you're capable of.

Copy assistant

Responsibilities

In addition to administrative duties, usually for the Department and Copy Chief, you will be responsible for maintaining records of what pages and projects have gone through the departments as part of the production process. You may be asked to line edit short copy and fact-check on credits as well.

Getting Hired

An interest in the written word, familiarity with the *Chicago Manual of Style* and/or *AP Style Manual* and a journalism or English background is key. Experience at a newspaper or internship is also a plus. Attention to detail and the ability to work long hours under deadline to get the job done are required.

Getting Promoted

Pitching in to lighten the load wherever you can here is the fastest way to a promotion; familiarity with your magazine's writing style and effective line editing will also give you a leg up in a year.

Research Assistant

Responsibilities

This is also called fact checking. You'll be responsible for the department's administrative duties as well as any research requests that come in from other editors. This department's responsibility is to be certain that every fact it publishes is correct. Your job will be to help them do that. This is great for someone who loves research and fact-finding.

Getting Hired

This is also not a backdoor position into another department and there is careful screening for that. A two-year commitment is usually preferred. Attention to detail and a great deal of follow-through are essential. Also have knowledge of Lexis-Nexis, Baseline and other research sources.

Getting Promoted

Being dedicated to tackling anything, from the longest features to the smallest reports, will help you rise quickly. Promotion is more an issue of being in the right place at the right time – i.e., whenever an opening comes up.

**Losing sleep over your job search?
Endlessly revising your resume?
Facing a work-related dilemma?**

Super-charge your career with Vault's newest career tools: Resume Reviews, Resume Writing and Career Coaching.

Vault Resume Writing

On average, a hiring manager weeds through 120 resumes for a single job opening. Let our experts write your resume from scratch to make sure it stands out.

- Start with an e-mailed history and 1- to 2-hour phone discussion
- Vault experts will create a first draft
- After feedback and discussion, Vault experts will deliver a final draft, ready for submission

Vault Resume Review

- Submit your resume online
- Receive an in-depth e-mailed critique with suggestions on revisions within TWO BUSINESS DAYS

Vault Career Coach

Whether you are facing a major career change or dealing with a workplace dilemma, our experts can help you make the most educated decision via telephone counseling sessions.

- Sessions are 45-minutes over the telephone

"I have rewritten this resume 12 times and in one review you got to the essence of what I wanted to say!"

– S.G. Atlanta, GA

"It was well worth the price! I have been struggling with this for weeks and in 48 hours you had given me the answers! I now know what I need to change."

– T.H. Pasadena, CA

"I found the coaching so helpful I made three appointments!"

– S.B. New York, NY

**For more information go to
www.vault.com/careercoach**

V/\ULT
> the insider career network™

Dream Jobs

CHAPTER 10

Here are some interesting stories of how some people got to where they are. One common link is a passion for what they do. They did it on their own merits, without connections, a family name or a coffer full of trust fund money. Their secrets? Hard work, patience and serendipity.

Independent film producer

Age: 31

Education: BA, English, Smith College

After finishing college, I used my school's alumni network through the career services center and moved to Los Angeles. I did a ton of informational interviews and started as a PA for *The Tonight Show*, which seems to be a landing point for lots of new arrivals to LaLa Land. I kept on interviewing and eventually landed a position at ABC as an assistant in sitcom development, which was the group that was looking for new sitcoms to air on the network. My boss was a nightmare and I didn't really like her, but it was a coveted job and she always reminded me of how many other applicants there were waiting for my position, so I stuck it out and made as many contacts as I could – especially at other networks and in talent agencies. I'd meet for late night drinks three or four nights a week to schmooze and maintain contacts with people. I initially tried going to lunch a couple of times, but my boss invariably called when I was out and I got in trouble.

I stayed 18 months at ABC when I heard of a position open at a production company in the Disney Studio lot – they were set to make the next Tom Cruise movie, so I put my name in the hat, interviewed and got the job. It sounds easy, but it was a lot tougher than that. I worked every angle I had – I dressed nicely, took the guy I knew at the company to fancy drinks and dinner (this on my assistant salary!), I offered to set him up with single girlfriends, I called other people and asked them to call on my behalf. Everything I could think of to make myself the coolest person in consideration.

I stayed at the job for several years, moving from director of development as one of the notorious D-girls, (young executive women working in television and film development) and then moved on to be a VP of development. I split off a few months ago with my Rolodex when one of the movies I really liked was passed over. I'm still committed to it, so I left, met with some financiers of smaller, independent production companies, got a B-list star attached and got the movie made. The work paid off because we're screening it at Cannes in the spring! I hope this will set me up to find more scripts and produce more movies on my own.

Senior vice president (strategic planning), major entertainment studio

Age: 35

Education: BA, Economics, Michigan; MBA, Wharton School at the University of Pennsylvania

After I graduated from college, I went into a pretty standard consulting job with Deloitte & Touche in Chicago, then left after a year to work as a staffer in Washington for my congressman. I was more interested in doing something in politics. Public policy was actually great preparation for Hollywood because it's all about selling your ideas to strangers who aren't really that interested in listening to you.

I applied to business school after a couple of years thinking I would return to Capitol Hill as a policy wonk, but got lured back into management consulting shortly thereafter. I ended up working with a firm with a substantial practice out on the West Coast. We were also one of the first consulting firms to actually have a full-fledged media practice. I found myself on a few projects over time that I found really intriguing. Barely one year out of business school, I nearly took the opportunity to run a small video game company, but it didn't seem to be the right decision at the time. After another year, I worked on a project with a major entertainment conglomerate and became pretty close to some of the senior executives there. Within a year, they made allusions to needing people. They never made any explicit offers or guarantees of hiring me, but I knew I was at least as competent and looked stronger on paper than many of their recent hires. I didn't want to offend my current bosses, so I quit and took some time off so as to not to violate my non-compete agreement, then came on board to the entertainment company six months later.

I've been here six years. I started as a manager working in the Theme Parks & Resorts division. We had a successful international launch, so I was able to get promoted to director within 18 months. At that point, I got involved with the company's Internet strategy, which was just taking off. We completed an acquisition that the CEO was really keen on, so I was promoted to vice president. There's a fair amount of turnover in the group, so when the Senior VP left to be the CEO of a media company in Northern California, I was promoted to that position.

Assistant publisher, major women's magazine

Age: 32

Education: BA, French, Duke

After college, I actually worked for about a year at Club Med in France, which was fun, but definitely not something for the long haul. I came back to the States, specifically to New York, where many of my friends were working, and initially was looking for a job in advertising. I sent my resume everywhere, had interviews with all the major agencies and lots of smaller ones, but wasn't able to land anything. This, despite the fact that it was the mid 1990s, the economy was booming AND advertisers had their highest billings ever! Without some creative background or a formal introduction, it was difficult to make it past the HR screen. And the alumni network from my college wasn't particularly useful for this industry.

I did get a break from one of the people I had interviewed with, however, who said that a friend who worked at a magazine was looking for a circulation assistant. I hadn't even considered magazine publishing or circulation, and the pay was certain to be a pittance. But times were tough, so I said what the heck, and gave it a go. It turned out that it was at a women's fitness publication.

Circulation, as it turned out, involved a combination of sales and marketing skills, which I turned out to be pretty good at. I quickly got the hang of selling to potential advertisers, learning the intricacies of direct mail and, best of all, I got along with my boss, who was one of the stars in the company.

I was promoted from circulation assistant to assistant circulation manager within two years. During that time, my boss was asked to head up the business side of a new startup celebrity magazine backed by one of the industry's publishing powerhouses. It was a brand new venture, so she went and asked me to come with her.

Literary agent

Age: 27

Education: BA, Psychology, UCLA

While I was in college, I worked on several student films and took tons of classes where I had the chance to meet other writers, directors and actors. I knew I wanted to be in the entertainment industry and, while I didn't get into UCLA Film School, I still knew that being in Los Angeles and at UCLA would be a great opportunity to take classes and meet people. I did semester internships all over the city at various production companies just to make contacts and meet people. I'd then keep in touch, taking people to coffee, sending little gifts, always asking them to keep me in mind if anything came up or to make introductions to others for me. And right after graduation, I got into a talent agency – of course in the proverbial mail room. I have to say, having started in the industry in college was an eye-opening experience – there were people in the mailroom with me who were in their 30s because they had just recently decided to pursue a career in the industry. That is one bit of advice I would give, especially for starting at an agency: if you have an interest, the best time to do it is when you're young, since it is pretty demeaning work.

I knew I would have to stick it out a while, but fortunately I had time. I was working on student films and scripts with some of my pals who were still in school, and I figured I would find another assistant position at a production company or within the agency in a year's time. I think a lot of people liked me, and by the time I had my one-year anniversary, most of my "mailroom class" had already quit. I was next up for a promotion to an agent's desk. I worked with the film agents, which turned out to be an awesome position. It was definitely abusive at times, and my first year was terrible, but I stayed on. After all, I knew it's what I wanted, and I was still only 23 years old.

While I knew I was reading some good scripts that should get some prominence, I started to understand that everything was dependent on who knew who, and giving people what they wanted. What I started to get really good at, which took me about a year to figure out, was to eavesdrop on phone calls. As an assistant, especially at an agency, you end up handling hundreds of calls a day, so you're sort of a switchboard operator of sorts. And I started to listen in on calls with huge A-list movie stars and directors. I started making friends with other assistants, especially the other enterprising ones at other studios who I knew were ambitious, and started getting the inside information about what was hot, so my boss could make a bid when the time was right. It's the inside information that makes you valuable. By having valuable info, and then threatening to take it somewhere else (say, to another agency, or another production company), they finally promoted me. They'll never promote you unless they have to. But once I had my own assistant, my own phone line and the ability to broker deals, I was able to start doing things for myself.

Screenwriter

Age: 30

Education: BA, English Literature, New York University

After college, I lived the life of a starving artist for several years, waiting tables and writing plays. I had a few off-off-off-Broadway productions that some friends and I ended up producing, but they were largely unsuccessful, short runs that were done exclusively for friends and friends of friends. By some twist of fate, I was able to get myself a literary agent who happened to come to one of the plays. It was a fortuitous thing because he turned out to be quite a shaker – though it also meant that I was one of 120 "clients" that he had. I tried being positive – at least he had more exposure to people who could potentially land me a job than I could.

I suppose the rest of the story is about luck. I had a breakfast meeting with my agent telling him of all the work that I had finished in recent months, not thinking anything of it. He just happened to go to a party later that week and talk to a producer who happened to be looking for a script on a courtroom drama. To this day, I'm not sure what the fixation on courtroom drama was about, but there it was. My agent happened to remember, don't ask me how, that the piece I mentioned off the cuff was a courtroom drama (they can be done very inexpensivcly with minimal set design) and sent over my script.

Turned out that it was actually something that the producer was interested in. He purchased it, and it languished for awhile, but then it was finally picked up again after some actors and a director agreed to be in it. Not only did the script actually give me some long-awaited financial help, but it also opened some doors for me into more regular television writing. In fact, for the coming TV season, I wrote a pilot episode that has been picked up by one of the major television networks.

Use the Internet's
MOST TARGETED
job search tools.

Vault Job Board

Target your search by industry, function, and experience level, and find the job openings that you want.

VaultMatch Resume Database

Vault takes match-making to the next level: post your resume and customize your search by industry, function, experience and more. We'll match job listings with your interests and criteria and e-mail them directly to your inbox.

VAULT
> the insider career network™

APPENDIX

FAQ

Glossary and Industry Jargon

Companies

Recommended Reading and Other Sources

FAQ

Are there specific organizations that will help me network?

Many universities have alumni networks with regular mixers and speeches on entering the industry. There are numerous classes at UCLA open to the public through the extension school which are also useful. One in particular, called Screenwriters on Screenwriting, has been held at the university for years. The annual book fair sponsored by the *Los Angeles Times* often brings in prominent members of the media, and there are numerous acting and screenwriting classes which, for a fee, are open to anyone and a great forum to meet fellow writers and others within the industry who may be able to lead to more connections.

Does an MBA really make a difference in media and entertainment?

For the creative side of the business, an MBA is largely irrelevant. There is a book called *Wannabe* that chronicles, via an engaging and entertaining story, the exploits of a Stanford MBA trying to make his way through the creative side of the entertainment industry. For the business side, strategic planning positions, consulting positions, banking and financing positions, an MBA is much more useful and will likely provide an edge over other candidates.

Are there "back-door" approaches that can work?

While it is possible, lateral moves are typically not very successful. There are exceptions, however. One famous Hollywood screenwriter tells a story of how he worked in the accounting division of Warner Brothers and, through some of the film financing discussions, became acquainted with some of the A-list producers whom he befriended and then slipped a script to. Active networking within any position is especially critical if you wish to transition from the business side to the creative side.

Family connections aside, what's the best way to break into creative?

Be an assistant. You can interview directly, or you can start making contacts by becoming a production assistant on a TV show, temping, doing informational interviews, taking classes or volunteering yourself to be a script reader. Another common bit of advice is to start young. The entertainment industry is fraught with superficiality and inequity – "it's harder to stomach the older you get," says one creative executive.

Are lateral moves within a company possible?

While difficult, lateral moves are not impossible. It largely depends on your relationship with others and the connections of your boss, who may be able to connect you with others. The main types of lateral moves are within businesses. Moves from business to creative or vice-versa are often difficult because the types of experience sought are very different. Within businesses, it is much more driven by who you know and can be strongly affected by the work that you have done.

Why are there so many producers listed at the end of a TV show or at the beginning of a movie? Who are all those people?

During the course of a project's completion, there are numerous individuals who become involved in bringing it to life. The level of involvement can range from first discovering the script and nurturing it through production, contributing money toward making the movie, initially casting the bid to purchase the rights to the script or book, discovering unique individuals who are able to bring the movie to life (e.g., breakout movie stars or an up-and-coming director). These individuals all ask to be recognized in some way with the release of the film and end up collecting various permutations of a "producer credit." Typically, the rule is that the later or further down a name appears, the less critical or more junior that person was in producing the project.

What is the difference between a manager and an agent? How do lawyers fit into the whole picture?

As one actor cheekily puts it, "The main difference is in how much of a cut they take from your paycheck." Agents typically get 10 percent, managers and lawyers often get less. An agent is usually a deal-doer, orchestrating someone's attachment to a film, television show, music production or other work of art and ensuring that the person receives the most money that he/she can. Managers generally have longer-term relationships with individuals, advising clients on career moves and longer-term strategic plans. Because the nature of an agent's relationship with his/her client is less involved, they often have more clients. Successful Hollywood managers usually have just a handful of clients. For many child stars, their parents serve as their managers. Lawyers look over the deals to ensure the best for their client. Many celebrities also have publicists, who get paid a small fee on a monthly basis to manage the individual press appearances and handle phone calls in the event of an emergency or mishap.

Where is the best place to find business jobs?

University networks are the best place to begin. Consulting firms that have business practices are also very useful. Going to work in consulting or banking, then going to business school and interviewing at entertainment companies is a good route.

What classes/universities are good preparation for the entertainment profession?

Schools in southern California are particularly useful. Other than that, any film classes or production experience that you can get that will enable you to have a tape, or some tangible evidence of work that you have done will be helpful. While people will rarely actually look at it, the fact that you have done it will usually be good enough to establish your interest in the field.

What is development?

The key players in the development stage are producers, screenwriters, agents and studio executives. Production companies, the homes of producers, receive hundreds of spec scripts (prospective movies) every year. The executives at the production companies then pick through the scripts (written by both new and established screenwriters), negotiate with agents to purchase interesting ones, then bring together key players (e.g., a director, lead actors, other producers) who will commit to starring in the film if a studio finances it. A studio is then "pitched" the idea and, if it approves, the film then gets a "green light" to go into production. The latter stage of development is also often called pre-production.

What is a spec script?

A spec script is something speculative, a version that is written without any upfront pay. In television, spec scripts are often written for shows that are already on-air.

What is A&R?

Artist and repertoire. These are the talent scouts that listen to demo tapes, attend shows, travel and keep their "ear to the ground" to understand new music and to uncover voices that best bring those trends to life.

Should I take the first job that I am offered to get my foot in the door or should I be selective?

If you have the financial resources to be picky, it is always best to strive for a "blue chip" opportunity – either at a top talent agency, production company or major studio. There are hundreds of small production companies that may give you opportunities, but unless you happen to be affiliated with a movie that gains some critical acclaim, it will be difficult (if not impossible) to parlay the position into something more substantial.

Does being in the entertainment industry mean that I have to live in New York or Los Angeles?

While the majority of entertainment and media jobs are in those two cities, there are opportunities in other areas as well.

Glossary and Industry Jargon

A&R: Artists and repertoires. A music industry term for "talent scouts" who look for new musicians for a record label to sign.

Ancillary revenue streams: Other ways for a company to generate revenue from customers other than its main source.

Cast: The "talent" (i.e. actors, actresses) who make up a production and perform for an audience

Convergence: The synthesis of various media vehicles to distribute content or enhance it (e.g. TV, film, music, Internet).

Crew: Those behind-the-scenes individuals who make a movie come to life; essentially all the people named except the cast when the credits roll after a TV show or movie.

Development: Often used together with the word hell. This is pre-pre-production, the state in which a script is being "shopped" around to various production companies and studios in the hopes that someone will want to make it into a movie.

D-girls: Twenty- and thirty-something women managers in Hollywood who have worked their way up through the assistant ranks.

Editorial calendar: A publishing term for the key articles that will appear in upcoming magazines; it is distributed to entice advertisers to commit to purchasing space in a publication.

Exhibitor model: The business model for film studios, in which a studio makes the movie, but then movie theaters (or exhibitors), which are separately owned, show them. Strategic planning executives often consider the wisdom of vertical integration by purchasing the theaters. Currently, theaters make money primarily on concessions, but also on some portion of the box office receipts (varies by studio).

Fire drills: Last-minute requests by bosses and managers to their subordinates, often requiring employees to stay late to complete the task; often used pejoratively, as fire drills are frequently a result of a manager ineffectively communicating with his colleagues.

Green light: When a creative executive approves a project to be taken to the next phase of execution, either filming of a movie or TV show, the recording of a record, the publishing of a book.

Glocalization: Adapting content from one market to another (e.g. MTV Asia, Spanish soap operas). The word is derived from combining globalization and localization.

Hollywood Creative Directory: A compendium of names, addresses and phone numbers of key agents, producers and other individuals in Hollywood and New York.

Legs: A term for a project's initial success upon launch, whereby marketing can be scaled back and incremental revenue can be driven by word of mouth. For example, if its opening weekend is strong, the movie will probably have legs.

Nielsens: Ratings of TV shows, used to determine a project's popularity as well as its advertising leverage.

Notes: Comments and suggestions by a creative executive to a writer on his/her script.

One-sheet: The film industry marketing term for movie posters that describe a movie, its stars and its plot.

Opening weekend: The eagerly anticipated initial few days of a film or record's release, from which the overall revenue it will generate are forecast.

Option: A small fee (as low as $1 and as much as several million depending on how coveted the piece is) usually paid to a writer, giving a producer exclusive rights to a book or script for a finite period of time (e.g. six months, one year).

Pass through rate: A publishing term for the number of individuals who read a magazine beyond its newsstand sales and subscriptions; for example, if a magazine is sent to a doctor's office and approximately 25 people read the magazine in a given month because it lies in the reception area, the pass-through rate is 25.

Pilot: A term in television for a single, initial episode of a new show. While scores of pilots are filmed by the networks every year, many bomb during audience testing or once they are aired.

Pitch: A pithy, verbal summary of a project given to potential producers or investors to entice them to move forward with the project. Usually a minute or less long.

Pre-production: The phase of a movie's life when the entire cast and crew is commissioned, the locations are scouted and the script is touched up. This is everything that happens after the movie has been "green lit" and before the first day of filming starts.

Property: An entertainment asset that forms the basis of other deals; for instance, *Harry Potter* and *The Lion King* are highly successful properties for Warner Brothers and Disney, respectively.

Release schedule: The calendar of films that will be launched at theaters on any given weekend.

Spec script: A film or television script written to showcase the writer's talents. In television, spec scripts are usually considered in order to get people cast as writers on TV shows. In film, spec scripts are occasionally purchased by studios to be made into movies.

Standards & Practices: This is a group, usually at the large television networks, that views all the content that airs on a network (including shows and commercials) to ensure that none of it "crosses the line," running the risk that the network could be sued or become the target of some vehement political activism.

Tentpoles: The major releases that occur during a movie studios release cycle. These films are typically anticipated to be the blockbusters driving a studio's annual revenues.

Three-picture deal: An agreement by which a director, writer or actor agrees to present their next three big projects to a particular studio first. The studio then has the "right of first refusal" – if it passes, then the individual can take the project somewhere else. Such deals are highly coveted, because they can be extremely lucrative for the individual without burdening him with the responsibility of delivering revenue.

Trade publishing: Mass market fiction and non-fiction that is sold in most bookstores. Distinct from academic textbooks and journals.

Trailer: The previews of upcoming films viewed at the beginning of a movie. There are specific "trailer houses" in Hollywood that specialize in creating these marketing vehicles.

Talent: The actors and musicians who appear in front of the camera or on stage.

VOD: Video-on-demand. The likely successor of home video and DVD, in which an individual will be able to see any movie at any time by using the TV remote control.

Employer Index

Miscellaneous Media

Blue Sky Animation
44 S. Broadway
White Plains, NY 10601
(914) 259-6500

Clear Channel Communications
200 East Basse Road
San Antonio, TX 78209
(210) 822-2828

Cox Communications
1400 Lake Hearn Drive, NE
Atlanta, GA 30319
(404) 843-5000

Digital Domain
300 Rose Avenue
Venice, CA 90291
(310) 314-2800

Dow Jones & Co.
200 Liberty Street
New York, NY 10281
(212) 416-2000

E.W. Scripps
312 Walnut Street
Cincinatti, CA 45202
(513) 977-3000

IMAX
2525 Speakman Drive
Mississauga, ON L5K 1
Canada
(905) 403-6500

Knight-Ridder
50 W. San Fernando St., Suite 1500
San Jose, CA 95113
(408) 938-7700

Liberty Media
12300 Liberty Blvd.
Englewood, CO 80112
(720) 875-5400

LucasFilm
San Rafael, CA
Fax (415) 662-5697

McGraw Hill
1221 Avenue of the Americas
New York, NY 10021
(212) 512-2000

New York Times Company
229 W. 43rd Street
New York, NY 10036
(212) 556-1234

Pixar
1200 Park Avenue
Emeryville, CA 94608
(510) 752-3000

Scholastic Corporation
557 Broadway
New York, NY 10012
(212) 343-6100

TiVo
2160 Gold Street
Alviso, CA 95002
(408) 519-9100

Miscellaneous Media, continued

Tribune Company
435 N. Michigan Avenue
Chicago, IL 60611
(312) 222-9100

Washington Post
1150 15th Street, NW
Washington, DC 20071
(202) 334-6000

Gaming

3DO
200 Cardinal Way
Redwood City, CA 94063
(650) 385-3000

Acclaim
One Acclaim Plaza
Glen Cove, NY 11542
(516) 656-5000

Activision
3100 Ocean Park Blvd.
Santa Monica, CA 90405
(310) 255-2000

Eidos
1 Hartfield Road
Wimbledon SW 193RU
London, UK
(212) 986-6667

Electronic Arts
209 Redwood Shores Parkway
Redwood City, CA 94065
(650) 628-1500

Infogrames
417 Fifth Avenue
New York, NY 10016
(212) 726-6500

Midway
2704 W. Roscoe Street
Chicago, IL 60618
(773) 961-2222

Nintendo of America
4820 150th Avenue NE
Redmond, WA 98052

Sega of America
650 Townsend Street, Suite 550
San Francisco, CA 94103-4908

THQ
27001 Aguora Road, Suite 375
Calabasas Hills, CA 91301
(818) 871-5000

Take Two
575 Broadway
New York, NY 10012
(212) 334-6633

TV Networks

ABC
77 W. 66th Street
New York, NY 10023
(212) 456-7777

CBS
51 W. 52nd Steet
New York, NY 10019
(212) 975-4321

NBC
30 Rockefeller Plaza
New York, NY 10112
(212) 664-4444

Fox
205 E. 67th Street
New York, NY 10021
(212) 452-5555

PBS
1320 Braddock Place
Alexandria , VA 22314
(703) 739-5000

A&E/History Channel
235 East 45th Streret
New York, NY 10071

Showtime/Movie Channel
1633 Broadway
New York, NY 10019

HBO/Cinemax
1100 Avenue of the Americas
New York, NY 10036

ESPN
ESPN Plaza
935 Middle Street
Bristol, CT 06010
(860) 585-2000

E!
5670 Wilshire Boulevard
Los Angeles, CA 90036

MTV/Nickelodeon/VH-1
1515 Broadway
New York, NY 10036

Univision
1999 Avenue of the Stars, Suite 3050
Los Angeles, CA 90067
(310) 556-7676

CNN
One CNN Center, Box 105366
Atlanta, GA 30348-5366
(404) 827-1500

BBC Wordlwide
80 Wood Lane
London, UK W12 OTT
020-8576-2000

Lifetime
309 W. 49th Street
New York, NY 10019
(212) 424-7000

Movie Studios and Music Labels

Disney
350 S. Buena Vista St.
Burbank, CA 91521
(818) 567-5000

MGM
2500 Broadway Street
Santa Monica, CA 90404
(310) 449-3000

Paramount
555 Melrose Avenue
Los Angeles, CA 90038
(213) 956-5000

Sony Pictures
10202 W. Washington Blvd.
Culver City, CA 90232
(310) 244-4000

20th Century Fox
10201 W. Pico Blvd.
Los Angeles, CA 90035
(310) 369-1000

Universal Studios
100 Universal City Plaza
Universal City, CA 91608
(818) 777-1000

Warner Brothers
4000 Warner Blvd.
Burbank, CA 91522
(818) 379-1850

Dreamworks SKG
100 Universal Plaza, Bldg. 10
Universal City, CA 91608
(818) 33-7700

Miramax Films
7966 Beverly Boulevard
Los Angeles, CA 90048
(323) 951-4200

New Line Cinema
116 N. Robertson Blvd., Suite 200
Los Angeles, CA 90048
(310) 854-5811

EMI Music Publishing
1290 Avenue of the Americas
New York, NY 10104
(212) 492-1200

Talent Agencies

Creative Artists Agency
9830 Wilshire Blvd.
Beverly Hills, CA 90212
(310) 288-4545

William Morris
One William Morris Place
Beverly Hills, CA 90212
(310) 859-4000

International Creative Management (ICM)
8942 Wilshire Blvd.
Beverly Hills, CA 90211
(310) 550-4000

United Talent Agency (UTA)
9560 Wilshire Blvd. Suite 500
Beverly Hills, CA 90212
(310) 273-6700

Endeavor
9701 Wilshire Blvd., 10th Floor
Beverly Hills, CA 90210
(310) 248-2000

The Gersh Agency
232 N. Canon Drive
Beverly Hills, CA 90210
(310) 274-6611

Movie Theater Companies

AMC/General Cinema
920 Main
Kansas City, MO 64105
(816) 221-4000

Century Theaters
150 Pelican Way
San Rafael, CA 94904
(415) 448-8400

Cinemark
3900 Dallas Parkway, Suit 500
Plano, TX 75093-7865
(972) 665-1000

Destination Theaters
4155 Harrison Blvd., Suite 210
Ogden, UT 84403
(801) 392-2001

Loews Cineplex
711 Fifth Avenue
New York, NY 10022-3109
(212) 833-6200

Mann Theaters
16530 Ventura Blvd., Suite 500
Encino, CA 91436
(818) 784-6266

Regal Cinemas
(also owns UA, Edwards)
7132 Regal Lane
Knoxville, TN 37918
(865) 922-1123

Production Companies

Brillstein-Grey Entertainment
9150 Wilshire Boulevard, Suite 350
Beverly Hills, CA 90212
(310) 275-6135

Jerry Bruckheimer Films
1631 Tenth Street
Santa Monica 90404
(310) 664-6262

Castle Rock Entertainment
335 N. Maple Drive, Suite 135
Beverly Hills, CA 90210-3867
(310) 285-2300

Icon Productions
5555 Melrose Avenue
Los Angeles, CA 90038
(323) 956-2100

Imagine Entertainment
9465 Wilshire Boulevard, 7th Floor
Beverly Hills, CA 90212
(310) 858-2000

Mandalay Pictures
5555 Melrose Avenue, Louis Building
Los Angeles, CA 90038
(323) 956-2400

Scott Rudin Productions
c/o Paramount Pictures,
5555 Melrose Avenue, DeMille Building, #100
Los Angeles, CA 90038
(323) 956-4600

Publishing Houses

Bantam Doubleday Dell Publishing Group
(part of Bertelsmann AG)
1540 Broadway
New York, NY 10036
(212) 354-6500

Chronicle Books
275 Fifth Street
San Francisco, CA 94103
(415) 537-3730

Harcourt Brace & Co.
15 E. 26th Street
New York, NY 10010
(212) 614-7850

HarperCollins
(subsidiary of NewsCorp)
10 E. 53rd Street
New York, NY 10022
(212) 207-7000

Hyperion
(division of Disney)
114 Fifth Avenue
New York, NY 10011
(212) 633-4400

Little, Brown & Co.
(part of Time Warner)
1271 Avenue of the Americas
New York, NY 10020
(212) 522-8700

Penguin U.S.A.
375 Hudson Street
New York, NY 10014
(212) 366-2000

Random House
201 E 50th Street
New York, NY 10022
(212) 751-2600

Simon & Schuster
(part of Viacom)
1230 Avenue of the Americas
New York, NY 10020
(212) 698-7000

St. Martin's Press
175 Fifth Avenue
New York, NY 10010
(212) 674-5151

Warner Books
(division of Time Warner)
1271 Avenue of the Americas
New York, NY 10020
(212) 522-7200

W. W. Norton & Company
500 Fifth Avenue
New York, NY 10010
(212) 354-5500

Recommended Reading and Other Sources

Books

Adventures in the Screen Trade: A Personal View of Screenwriting and Hollywood, by William Goldman (Warner Books, 1989). The acclaimed screenwriter of *The Princess Bride* gives surprisingly relevant advice on making it in the industry. Included in the text is the screenplay for *Butch Cassidy and the Sundance Kid.*

A Passion to Win, by Sumner Redstone (Simon & Schuster, 2001). The backstory behind the making of Viacom, parent company of MTV, VH1 and Nickelodeon.

Hollywood Creative Directory. Though expensive (each guide retails for $60), this annually printed guide is a must-have list of agents, managers, production companies and distributors with names, addresses, phone numbers and contact information for anyone looking for contacts or leads in the industry.

Hello, He Lied: And Other Truths from the Hollywood Trenches, by Linda Obst (Broadway Books, 1997). The at-times amusing and autobiographical story of Ms. Obst, one of the producers of *Flashdance* and *Sleepless in Seattle.*

Hit & Run: How Jon Peters and Peter Guber Took Sony for a Ride in Hollywood, by Nancy Griffin and Kim Masters (Touchstone, 1997). The hilarious true story of the debauchery and excesses of two legendary studio executives.

Story: Substance, Structure, Style & the Principles of Screenwriting, by Robert McKee (HarperCollins, 1997). While this is more relevant for screenwriters, McKee holds regular workshops for development executives to instruct them on the intricacies of strong story-telling. He's widely regarded as the master of this sort of stuff.

The Big Deal: Hollywood's Million-Dollar Spec Script Market, by Thom Taylor (William Morrow & Co., 1999). One of Oliver Stone's former employees tells juicy tales of the backstory behind how some of the biggest movies of the last two decades (e.g. *Total Recall, Alien, In the Line of Fire, Seven*) actually got made.

The Hollywood Job Hunter's Survival Guide, by Hugh Taylor (Lone Eagle, 1993). Written by a former assistant, this manual is a must for anyone entering the creative side of the business.

The Movie Business Book, by Jason Squire (editor) (Fireside, 1992). An excellent overview of various parts of the film industry (production, distribution, video, licensing) told in a combination of technical detail and accessible tone by industry experts.

The Writer's Journey: Mythic Structure for Writers, by Christopher Vogler (Michael Wiese Productions, 1992). This is a how-to-screenwrite classic that sits on the bookshelves of development executives everywhere.

You'll Never Eat Lunch in this Town Again, by Julia Phillips (Signet, 1992). Scathing expose dishing tales of Hollywood dirt.

Wannabe: A Would-Be Player's Misadventures in Hollywood, by Everett Weinberger (St. Martin's Press, 1997). A Stanford Business School grad recounts his first person account of trying to break into the creative side of the film industry after finishing his MBA.

Work in Progress, by Michael Eisner and Tony Schwartz (Random House, 1998). The Disney CEO reveals some opinionated and controversial points of view about the entertainment industry in this recent memoir.

Videos

Swimming with Sharks. Kevin Spacey brings to life the nightmare that is every creative assistant's boss in this hilarious farce of trying to break into the entertainment industry. Frank Whaley plays his unlucky assistant.

The Big Picture. This spoof stars Kevin Bacon as a hyped film student who snakes his way around Hollywood in his first big feature film.

The Player. Robert Altman classic that has Tim Robbins as a young studio executive tormented by a mysterious screenwriter.

Independent's Day. A documentary of what goes on behinds-the-scenes at the Sundance Film Festival.

Web sites

Internet Movie Database. A subsidiary of Amazon.com, IMDB.com has come to be one of the most trusted resources of movie buffs, creative executives and trivia seekers everywhere. The database has cast, crews and bios on nearly every English-language movie (and many foreign language films too) ever made.

Cinemedia.org. Self-proclaimed to be the "Internet's largest film and media directory" with over 25,000 links.

Whorepresents.com. A database of talent agents and clients they represent.

Film Schools

Actor's Studio Drama School
66 W. 12th Street, 6th Floor
New York, NY 10011
(212) 229-5859

American Film Institute
2021 North Western Avenue
Los Angeles, CA 90027
(323) 856-7600

New York University – Cinema Studies
721 Broadway, 6th Floor
New York, NY 10003-6807
(212) 998-1600

UCLA – School of Film, Television and Digital Media
Box 951622
Los Angeles, CA 90095.
E-mail: info@tft.ucla.edu

USC – School of Cinema – Television
University Park Campus
Los Angeles, CA 90089
(213) 740-1111

Groups and Organizations

Academy of Motion Pictures Arts and Sciences
The non-profit that disseminates the annual Oscars.

8949 Wilshire Blvd
Los Angeles, CA 90211
(310) 247-3000 • www.oscars.org

American Cinema Foundation
Non-profit to support new filmmakers.

9911 West Pico Blvd., Suite 510
Los Angeles, CA 90035.
(310) 286-9420 • www.cinemafoundation.com

British Film Institute
The UK's largest cinema-related non-profit.

21 Stephan Street
London W1T 1LN, UK
44 (0)20 7255 1444 • www.bfi.org.uk

Director's Guild of America
Resources for directors, aspiring directors and other creative types.

7920 Sunset Blvd.
Los Angeles, CA 90046
(310) 289-2000 • www.dga.org

Motion Picture Association of America
Group that distributes film ratings.

15503 Ventura Blvd.
Encino, CA 91436
(818) 995-6600 • www.mpaa.org

Museum of TV and Radio
Has branches in both New York and Los Angeles. In addition to the opportunity to view virtually all old TV and radio programs ever made, the museum has regular appearances and seminars that are open to the public featuring writers, directors, and others involved in the creative process.

465 N. Beverly Drive
Beverly Hills, CA 90210
(310) 786-1025

25 West 52 Street
New York, NY
(212) 621-6800

National Film Board of Canada
Canadian non-profit with robust resources for aspiring filmmakers.

350 West 5th Avenue, Suite 4820
New York, NY 10118
(212) 629-8890 • www.nfb.ca

Screen Actor's Guild
Union of actors providing resources for actors.

5753 Wilshire Blvd.
Los Angeles, CA 90036
(323) 954-1600

1515 Broadway, 44th Floor
New York, NY 10036
(212) 944-1030

ShoWest
Cinema exhibitors annual convention.

777 Broadway, 5th Floor
New York, NY 10003
(646) 654-7680 • www.showest.com

Writer's Guild of America
Provides resources for Hollywood screenwriters and playwrights, as well as programs for non-writers.

7000 West 3rd Street
Los Angeles, CA 90048
(323) 951-4000 • www.wga.org

Women in Film
Non-profit to nurture and support women in the film industry.

8853 West Olympic Blvd., Suite 201
Los Angeles, CA 90211
(310) 657-5144 • www.wif.org

About the Author

Sucharita Mulpuru: Sucharita moved to Los Angeles just after graduation from college to pursue a career in the entertainment industry. While taking screenwriting classes at UCLA, she started work as an analyst in the Strategic Planning group at the Walt Disney Company.

While at Disney, Sucharita spent time at talent agencies, production companies and movie studios to pursue a creative career in show business. She later went back to business during the dot-com bubble, where she helped to create an online retailer called Estyle. She completed her undergraduate degree at Harvard University and her MBA at Stanford. Other companies she has worked with include the Zagat Survey, General Motors and Intuit. She contributes to *Business Week Online*, has authored a novel and travel guide to Europe and has completed several television and feature length screenplays. She currently lives in San Francisco with her husband.

Use the Internet's
MOST TARGETED
job search tools.

Vault Job Board

Target your search by industry, function, and experience level, and find the job openings that you want.

VaultMatch Resume Database

Vault takes match-making to the next level: post your resume and customize your search by industry, function, experience and more. We'll match job listings with your interests and criteria and e-mail them directly to your inbox.

VAULT
> the insider career network™

VAULT CAREER GUIDES
GET THE INSIDE SCOOP ON TOP JOBS

"Cliffs Notes for Careers"

– FORBES MAGAZINE

Vault guides and employer profiles have been published since 1997 and are the premier source of insider information on careers.

Each year, Vault surveys and interviews thousands of employees to give readers the inside scoop on industries and specific employers to help them get the jobs they want.

"To get the unvarnished scoop, check out Vault"

– SMARTMONEY MAGAZINE

VAULT